Chonda Pierce says...

"Sally is a friend of mine and like all good friends, we love to talk! Her book reads just like a fun and tender conversation with your BFF - extremely engaging and witty. Grab a cup of coffee and enjoy! I not only recommend her book, her performances, her chocolate-chip cookies -- I recommend her friendship! She always makes me laugh!"

> ~ Chonda Pierce, comedian and author of
> *On Her Soapbox, Second Row Piano Side,* and
> *Laughing in the Dark*

♥

Ken Davis says...

"Sally Baucke is a master of laughter. Her hilarious observations of everyday life help us see life in a brighter light. Do not drink hot beverages or operate heavy machinery while reading this book!"

> ~ Ken Davis, comedian, inspirational speaker,
> and author of *Fully Alive, Happily Ever Laughter:*
> *Discovering the Lighter Side of Marriage,* and
> *Lighten Up! Great Stories from One of America's*
> *Favorite Storytellers*

♥

Judy Carter says...

"Filled with LOL moments and great life affirming takeaways. I laughed so hard my Spanx rolled down."

> ~ Judy Carter, motivational humorist and author
> of *The Comedy Bible* and *The Message of You:*
> *Turn Your Life Story into a Money-Making*
> *Speaking Career*

Nina Roesner says...

"I needed some laughter in my life as a mom, a daughter, and a wife…Sally's book hit the spot! She made me smile, and then she made me laugh so hard I cried. It's nice to know that other women have dealt with some of the same things I have, and can find humor in them. I recommend it highly for any woman who needs to take a moment to not take herself and her life so seriously!"

> ~ Nina Roesner, author of *The Respect Dare* (Thomas Nelson, 2012)

♥

Dr. Kevin Leman says...

"Sally is as funny on the page as she is on the stage! Don't miss this Laugh Out Loud read!"

> ~ Dr. Kevin Leman, psychologist and author of *The Birth Order Book, Have a New Kid by Friday, Sheet Music,* and *What A Difference A Mom Makes*

WHAT didn't kill me MADE ME ~~stronger~~ Funny!

Sally Baucke

What Didn't Kill Me Made Me ~~Stronger~~ Funny!
Copyright © 2013 by Sally Baucke
Strong House Press

ISBN 978-1490484129

Cover Design: Gwene Daugherty Design
Cover Photography: Shane Harden Photography
Sally Logo: Kim Jorden Designs

Printed in the United States of America

"He who laughs...lasts."
~ Erma Bombeck

"Nietzsche famously said
'Whatever doesn't kill you makes you stronger,'
But what he failed to stress is
that it almost kills you."
~ Conan O'Brien

A cheerful heart is good medicine.
~ God (Proverbs 17:22 NIV)

Table of Contents

Acknowledgements

Years ago, I was told that all good speakers should write a book. That made as much sense to me as saying all good gymnasts should be able to sew leotards. However, after deciding that an official protest would be useless, I set out to produce a manuscript that people would not only enjoy reading, but would reflect what I do on stage. Unfortunately for me, writing the way I talk made me sound like Yoda (hmmm...kill me, it did...funny, it was). Easy it was not.

Thankfully, I improved as a writer, but not without a little help from my friends. For their many contributions to this painstaking process, I sincerely wish to thank Gwene Daugherty, Jenn Doucette, Crista Vest Lienhart, Nina Roesner, Jill Savage, Sara Spencer, and Mary Kay Smith. You have helped me find my voice, my message, and my words.

Most of all, I need to thank my dearest friend, Carol Walters Heath, who, out of love and loyalty, has read countless drafts of this manuscript over the last three years. (Yes, it took me three years. That pesky real life kept getting in the way.) Not only did she read them all, she made note of every single laugh out loud moment, and she never laughs out loud when she reads (or so she says). That cheered me on in a way nothing else could have.

I'd also like to thank my devoted husband, Craig (aka Fred), who is proficient in both editorial input and encouragement. The fact that you believed I could do this gave me the confidence to finish the task (besides the fact that you told me it was time to wrap it up so you didn't have to keep eating frozen pizza for dinner). I love you for that. There's no one I'd rather spend the rest of my days laughing with than you.

And finally, to my quiver full of blessings: Spencer, Cooper, and Camden. You fill my life with joy. You have always been, and will always be, my favorite audience ever. ♥

Introduction

The ~~Funny~~ Thing About Disappointment

I was supposed to have been born Greek, I just know it. I love the whole Big Fat Greek Wedding thing. Greeks have large extended families who know everything about you, are always up in your business, and stick together like glue. There are always dozens of cousins who hug each other with gusto and are there with love and support (and a plate of yummy comfort food) when you need it most. Greeks are also superior in that they have the best hair on the planet, thick with natural curl and body.

To the contrary, my family tree is smallish, with only a few cousins, and not a natural curl among us. We see each other occasionally, hug politely, and the closest we come to Greek-like gusto is singing loudly around the piano at Christmas. Very few of them were at my wedding. I'm sure they would have come if we had lived on the same side of the Mason-Dixon Line, but I'm from Chicago, and that's a hard line to cross, in more ways than one. They are all lovely Southerners, as are my parents, which makes me a "damnYankee." It was years before I realized that was two words instead of one.

Rather than being born in Greece, as I should have been, I was born in Japan, although you couldn't tell that by looking at me. I was born in Okinawa, Japan on a U.S. Air Force Base. Consequently, I was asked two questions on a routine basis:

1) Can I legitimately become President of the United States, and
2) Am I Japanese?

I never looked into it because everyone knows that Presidents are notorious for greying prematurely. You can simply refer to the front of this book to grip the hilarity of the second question. I am 5'7", with blond hair and green eyes. I speak perfect English, have a thick Chicago accent, and am a total klutz with chopsticks.

However, my Consular Report of Birth (a piece of paper the U.S. military hands out instead of a regular birth certificate when you are born on an international base) identifies my homeland as Okinawa, Japan. When I got my driver's license, I was told to stand in the "alien" line, even though my U.S. certificate was prominently displayed in my hand. It was like WW II, except that I doubt many blond-haired, green-eyed gals were thrown into the Japanese prison camps. My father had said to hang on to that piece of paper because if I lost it, I might as well not be an American. Apparently, having it doesn't make much difference.

On paper, I am Japanese; but in reality, I am Scotch Irish, with a touch of English. That would explain my love of *Braveheart*, plaid skirts, and all things Royal, especially Princess Diana.

Oh how I loved the Princess of Wales. She was my kind of gal. For example, she preferred sunny vacations on a boat, albeit hers was a luxury yacht (something I've never been on) and I'm more of a pontoon girl, but who's comparing. She wasn't a fan of camping. How do I know this? She was the most photographed woman in the world. If she'd gone camping we would have seen it. She probably felt about camping like I do: it's real life made harder. Catch my own food? Gather sticks to make a fire just so I can heat up my tea? No thank you.

In addition, Diana loved beautiful clothes and sparkly things, both fascinations I share with the Princess. Luckily for her, she had fabulous gems to choose from daily. (None of hers were from Claire's, but again, who's comparing.) She also had a thick head of beautiful blond hair which looked salon-perfect in every photo. Of course, someone else did her hair for her every single day of her life, *including the back,* something I could only aspire to in my wildest dreams.

For all her Royal perks, Diana seemed kind and down to earth. There was something approachable and familiar about her that made the whole world fall in love with the lovely princess, myself included. She had her share of disappointments like any other human being, and she shared them openly. Diana loved ballet, and always wanted to be a ballerina. Sadly, she lamented that her tall figure didn't allow it. Are you kidding me? I would have given anything for her statuesque frame and long legs. However, I felt her angst. I always wanted to be a supermodel, but my short legs and long torso make me the equivalent of a human Bassett Hound, an undesirable combination for would-be runway models. (I am the same height sitting as I am standing, a demonstrable fact.) Isn't it funny how everyone, even Princesses, always want something they don't have.

Despite our inseam differences, HRH and I had a lot in common. She was naïve, married young, and was misunderstood by her mother-in-law, whom she tried desperately to impress. Most of all, Diana and I were kindred spirits because she adored her boys more than anything on the planet. When she died, I felt like I'd lost a sister.

So what does a gal do when she doesn't feel as though her life fits who she really is or what she desires to be? She pretends she is someone else. At least, that's what I did, even if only for a few moments here and there.

When I was a kid, I watched shows like the *Brady Bunch*, the *Partridge Family*, and *Little House on the Prairie* with religious fervor. I felt as though the characters were distant relatives sending messages through subspace. (OK, so you can't send subspace messages from the prairie, but you know what I mean.) I wanted to be part of either one of those families. They weren't Greek, but they were a lot closer to it than my family was.

Being a Brady would have been awesome because any family with six kids and a live-in maid named Alice was automatically way cooler than mine. To my knowledge, they weren't Greek, but they acted like it, and that was enough for me.

The Partridge Family was even more attractive. There were a lot of kids, and they all had musical ability. They did normal family stuff, but in addition, they also sang together, wore matching velvet pantsuits, and traveled on a multi-colored bus. As a total extrovert, I would have died to have been able to do that with my family. I watched with keen interest as eldest daughter Laurie (played by Susan Dey) exchanged knowing glances onstage with their TV mother Shirley Jones while they sang. Even the sarcastic quips between the always-irritating Danny* (Bonaduce) and his siblings made me envious of their cohesive unit, bound by inside jokes and an obvious affection for one another. Unfortunately, my sarcastic quips were never met with quite the same

---

* *I am always perplexed when a character's name on a show is the same as the actor's name in real life. Is it too confusing for them or what? Hello. That's why they call it acting.*

enthusiasm as Danny's were, but he had the benefit of a laugh track.

The family I longed to be in most, however, was the Ingalls family in their warm and welcoming Little House on the Prairie. *I wanted to be* Laura Ingalls Wilder. I dreamt about living in their austere lean-to, even though it was on a desolate wasteland without a single mall nearby. I'm a city girl at heart, but for reasons best left to mental health professionals, I was attracted to a lifestyle that included wearing gingham dresses that were washed by hand in a nearby stream. Neither Diana nor I would ever dream of wearing those ugly white bonnets to bed like Laura and her sisters did, but the sense of family closeness would have been worth the bonnet-head we would undoubtedly have woken up with.

In all honesty, my longing went much deeper than the lunch pail Laura carried to her one-room schoolhouse. While I couldn't put a finger on it at the time, I was jealous of Laura's family dynamics, especially her relationship with her Pa. She was secure in his love, even when he was disappointed in something she'd done. Pa adored Laura so much he even gave her a pet name, Half-Pint, something I always wished I had. My dad often called me "Wild Child," which didn't exactly have the same affectionate ring to it.

As if being born a century too late, with no nickname and the wrong nationality weren't enough, I've lived in the wrong time zone for the last two decades. In the Eastern Time zone, our news comes on at 11:00 pm instead of the ten o'clock spot I was used to. That wouldn't be a problem if we, as a collective time zone, were compensated with an extra hour of beauty sleep to make up for the lost shut-eye. But noooo…it doesn't work that way. Our day starts the same time as everybody else in the country. No wonder people stereotype Easterners as less friendly; we're sleep-deprived from staying up to watch the weather man tell us whether it's going to rain or not during our bleary-eyed commute to Starbucks.

It's even worse for those of us who like to laugh ourselves to sleep, because everyone else's "Late Show" is our "Middle of the Night Show." I don't need to tell the rest of you night owls that staying up late has it's price.

I was furious about the time inequity and certain that there was a "higher up" I could petition to see if it was possible to change the whole time zone set-up. What a futile protest that was (something about international datelines and Greenwich Village time, yada yada yada). The whole conversation went nowhere. Diana would have gotten someone's attention, but I certainly didn't. Fortunately, it's not as big an issue as it once was. Thanks to the ingenuity of Al Gore I can get my news from the World Wide Web any time I want.

So, like Al, if you can change something for the better, go for it. I'm all for positive change. However, there are invariably a few (and sometimes more than a few) unpalatable situations in life which cannot be changed no matter how hard we try. I don't care what the headlines and bylines read *(Live the Most Fantastic Life! or You: Controlling the Universe!)*; there simply are circumstances beyond anyone's control. I hate those situations. They frustrate the heck out of me because I'm a problem solver. I want to fix things, reverse them, or opt out of the situation altogether if a solution can't be found.

If I can't solve it, change it, or get out of it, I do the next best thing, which is to complain about it. After all, technically, complaining is a form of "doing something" (at least, in the mind of the complainer). Unfortunately, complaining rarely helps anything. In fact, it usually makes the situation worse (especially in the mind of the complainer).

The weather is a perfect example of this. I've heard weather forecasters refer to snow as though it were nuclear fallout instead of faceted crystals of frozen water. What does that accomplish? Nothing. Complaining about snow doesn't bully it into falling somewhere else. Relentless griping has no power to warm up the atmosphere, turning Suzy Snowflake into Randy Raindrop.

The only thing complaining does is take away from the beauty of seeing snow for what it really is: free (albeit cold) decoration for the earth. I love snowflakes, by the way. I do, however, take issue with the silly proclamation that "no two snowflakes are alike." Really? Has anyone checked every last one before they thaw? I don't think so.

Snow has a lot of perks. It blankets the ugly brown winter ground and sparkles in the sun like diamonds, and who doesn't like sparkly things? It's an Extreme Earth Makeover from the heavens, even though it means you now have to wear thick down coats that make you look like a cow. So why not embrace, even celebrate the glittery white fluff as it descends?   OK, so sometimes snow causes multi-car accidents and makes you even later for work than the stupid time zone, but the point here is that to grumble about things that I have no control over only highlights the negative.

Ultimately, griping only serves to make me miserable, as well as those around me. I do have one exception to the griping clause. Really thick, disgusting humidity can turn even the best hair day into put-a-bag-over-your-head-you-look-like-a-troll day.   (I am a self-proclaimed hair-a-tic. Not heretic. There's a definite difference.) So in light of my quest for perfect hair, I reserve the right to complain about humidity all day, every day.

If huffing and puffing actually changed something, I would consider it worth my time. It doesn't, and so it's not. I've spent a lot of time in a therapist's office huffing and puffing about things I desperately wished I could change. As it turns out, most of the things I complained so hard about were never in my control to begin with. It has taken years of retrospection, as well as very intense introspection, to understand that all the huffing and puffing in the world will never "fix" anything. I can never "fix" everything. And all the complaining in the world will never transform me into a Greek Princess, a slender long-legged beauty, or a beloved little prairie girl on Central Time.

The wonderful news is that, while my past has its share of disappointments (and let's face it, whose doesn't), I have a choice about what to do with those disappointments. So do you. I can wail...or wag. Repeat...or repair. Crack...or crack up. It's like "they" say (I don't know who "they" are but they were my grandmothers' most quoted source of inspiration), you can either laugh or cry. Crying has certain benefits, but it makes my face red and blotchy. It also ruins my expensive under-eye concealer, which I refuse to apply more than once a day simply out of principle.

So if I'm not gonna cry, and I refuse to reapply, that leaves me with only one option: I choose to laugh. Yes, I am going to laugh. Laughter is a happier, healthier choice, plus it doesn't mess with my mascara. (Waterproof does not necessarily mean tear-proof, a rather misleading concept if you ask me.) Laughter may not transform the problem, but it transforms my attitude, and that changes the way I live my life. In other words, laughter has the ability to change *me,* even if it doesn't change the circumstance.

We've all heard the saying "what doesn't kill you makes you stronger." Yeah, yeah, right. Sure, it's a positive message about enduring life's bumps and bruises, but it isn't the whole picture, at least in my book (no pun intended). I don't want to just survive; I want to *thrive,* and laughter helps me do that.

When I say laughter, I am not talking about "knock knock who's there" funny. I mean "funny you should say that" funny, or "life is funny that way" funny.

To me, funny is a noun as well as an adjective. Funny is the sweet coating that makes a salty moment palatable. After all, sweet and salty snacks are a lot like life. Sweet moments are great, but it takes a saltier bite to appreciate the sugary sweetness. Once the savory salt becomes overwhelming, the sweet rushes back in to soothe the salty soul. Life really is like a box of chocolates, I agree, but I can narrow it down even further than the affably daft Mr. Gump. Life is like a Reese's peanut butter cup, with all it's glorious sweet and salty moments, just waiting to be unwrapped.

Yes, life's less-than-stellar moments have forced me to wise up and lighten up. Most of all, they've taught me to look Up. There's a proverb in Scripture (a truly trustworthy source of advice) that says "a cheerful heart is good medicine." To that I say Up. The. Dose. (My three favorite words in the English language.) Why? Because laughter is a gift from God, a very tangible present with an amazing ability to soothe the past. Now that I think of it, my favorite gifts have always been wrapped up in the funny papers.

I've heard it said that comics use laughter to soothe their wounded souls. Well, that's probably accurate to some extent, at least based on the comedians I've run across, including myself. (Well, I haven't exactly run across myself in person, just in my head, but....ok, need I say more?) If that's the case, we are some of the luckiest people in the world. There are times where laughter is the only thing that's gotten me through (besides chocolate, don't forget the chocolate), and I'm thankful to have it.

I'm pretty sure I'm not alone. You know what "they" say…"when life gives you lemons, make lemonade." Well, forget that. Just have the cruise director put the lemons in my Diet Coke while I laugh my way to the Greek isles in search of my wavy-haired Royal relatives. By the way, does anyone know what time zone Greece is in ?

Chapter 1

There's No Whining In
~~Baseball or~~ Childhood

"Because nobody goes through life without a scar."
Carol Burnett

My favorite scene in *A League of Their Own* is when Tom Hanks' character declares "there's no crying in baseball." While never caught on film, I am almost certain my father made a similar statement of disgust in regards to whining before I was even brought home from the hospital. As far back as I can remember, whining was simply not permitted in our household, and I mean <u>never</u>. My dad served as a fighter pilot in the U.S. Air Force and ran our home like a miniature version of the military, except that enlistment wasn't voluntary. I was drafted at birth. We were fully expected to fall into rank at home. The more disciplined I was, the happier he was. I even made pathetic little-girl salutes when he walked in the door just to see him smile.

Whining was *so* discouraged that at times I wondered if our home had been officially declared a "WFZ" by the government. (WFZ stands for Whine Free Zone. The government never does anything without using abbreviations that no one else understands.) Perhaps my dad was just following orders. Maybe it was a top secret mandate, or a covert designation on a map in the basement of the Pentagon. I couldn't be sure. So even when I was tempted to whine, I never did, just in case Big Brother was listening. Heaven forbid that a SWAT team came crashing onto our front lawn and my whining was to blame. There weren't enough cute salutes in the world to counteract that breach of intelligence, not to mention the cost a full SWAT assault would incur. I could kiss my allowance good-bye for…forever.

Apparently, whining was not encouraged in the military, and understandably so. After all, we wouldn't have a very effective militia if soldiers were allowed to complain. "Sorry General, I'd rather not participate. I'm just not feeling it." Can you imagine a General droning on and on in a loud nasal voice to the Commander-in-Chief "C'mooooon Mr. President! I dropped the bomb yesterday. Can't somebody else drop it today? Why is it always my turn?" No, me neither.

My father wasn't allowed to whine (or complain, for that matter), so we weren't allowed to whine (or complain) either. The natural result of any mandate is that it creates an inevitable domino effect. For example, once a person becomes fully indoctrinated into the militant No-Whining Club, there is zero tolerance for anyone else who whines, similar to a lifelong smoker who kicks the habit and is intolerant of anyone blowing smoke in their general direction. In other words, if *they* can't smoke, *you* can't smoke.

Since whining was off limits for me, I couldn't stand it in anyone else either, especially other children. Children who were allowed to whine disgusted me. I could stop whining on a dime, why couldn't they? Circumstances were irrelevant. Resistance was futile. Whining was verboten, no matter the situation. Such a strict policy seemed a little harsh, especially in a toy store where whining is practically expected, but looking back, I'm rather glad he put the kibosh on that behavior. Some people never outgrow that habit, and nobody likes a whiner. I guess in this case Father really did know best.

I wasn't much of a soldier, but Father Fatigues did his best to instill many valuable traits and skills in me. The most surprisingly beneficial skill is something most men would give their right arm for the women in their lives to possess. I'm talking about the ability to "get ready to go" in a short amount of time. My dad's military training taught him that, and he passed it on to me. Thanks to him, I can get out of the house faster than anyone I have ever known, male or female, including Batman, and he had the benefit of a Bat pole.

I know women who've spent half their lives (and a whole lot of their income) in the name of "getting ready." Anyone who endorses a 35-step makeup regimen is not someone I can relate to. I could never vacation with someone like that because we would never be ready at the same time. I simply can't justify taking that much time to put stuff on my face that I will have to turn around and wash off in 16 hours or less. Not a great return on investment, time-wise.

Besides, I never witnessed that kind of primping as a kid. My mother is a natural beauty who can get away with very little cosmetic spackle and paste. She always touted the benefits of a simplistic "get and go" style, and I soon learned why. When my father said it was "time to get up and go," it was TIME TO GET UP AND GO. It was that simple.

As a result, by the time I was eight years old, I knew how to jump in the shower, dry off, pull on my clothes, and brush my teeth (always rinsing the foamy spit in the sink or else it didn't count). I was not allowed to leave without doing "something decent" with my hair*, so I quickly styled it while I hunted for my shoes. (If I couldn't put my hands right on them it meant they weren't lined up in my closet like they were supposed to be, an inexcusable cause for delay.) I was able to do all that, and skip out the door in ten minutes flat, nine if I didn't shave my legs. I didn't start shaving my legs until I was eleven or twelve, and I've always wondered what step suffered when I did start shaving, but I've never figured that out. It certainly wasn't my hair, because I never even did the back.

So with our less-is-more and out-the-door motto, it only made sense that I knew how to be presentable in public with the speed of a fighter pilot scrambling to his cockpit. I've never actually been called on to do so, but if I ever were, you can bet my hair would be

---

My mother always warned me against having hair that "looked like a rat's nest." To this day I have never seen a rat's nest and would be surprised if my prim and proper mother ever has either. How she knew to alert me to such a travesty is beyond me.

"decent," and my breath would be minty fresh when I took off.

Even though I never joined the "real military" (at least I haven't seen any *official* paperwork), I was thankful for my dad's insistence on military readiness. That little trick has come in handy in the civilian world on more than one occasion.

Every family has some sort of rule book they live by. There were the normal run-of-the mill parental rules such as "the phone is not a toy" or "clean up your room." Those are for amateurs. A professional-grade military family was expected to carry out a much more strenuous routine, if for no other reason than to make life more difficult.

Military "brats," as we were called (again, not the nickname I was looking for), knew the drill. Military life had a lot of rules, many of which spill over into family life. Most rules mandated good behavior, i.e., yes ma'am, no ma'am, yes sir, no sir, that type of thing. Children were to be respectful and only give answers in a yes-or-no format, something I desperately wish politicians were required to do. We also knew never to question the orders given by a commanding officer, which, as it would happen to be, was my father. Saluting was optional, but not entirely discouraged.

In addition to behavior rules, our family had an entirely different set of rules that fell under the category of "responsible homeownership rules." These mandates were designed to keep furniture from wearing, utilities from skyrocketing, and children from having fun, or so it seemed. These rules included, but were not limited to:

- *Shoes left out can (and will) be thrown away.*

- *Never, ever leave toothpaste in the sink (even if that means scraping it off with your fingernail).*

- *Never put your feet up on the sofa (that's what the floor is for).*

- *Never touch the carpet with your feet (tricky at best).*

- *Never eat in the car (chewing gum counts as food).*

- *Never slam the car door when exiting the vehicle (Note to self: carry an anemometer* at all times).*

- *Never ask for a ride if you can walk the distance (until the wind chill drops to the point that your spit freezes, then you can call for a ride).*

- *Never touch the walls with your hands or body. (Takes some concentration, but it can be done.)*

- *Never secure anything on the wall using nails, glue, push pins, scotch tape, velcro, or gum. It will ruin the paint. (Decoration is overrated.)*

- *If you are cold, put more clothing on (but not so many layers that you rub up against the walls and door frames).*

- *Do not touch anything that does not belong to you (and most things do not belong to you).*

- *If you moved something put it back exactly where*

---

* *An anemometer is a scientific device used to gauge wind speed. Wind speed in Chicago is variable, and it is often a factor in the rate and volume at which a car door slams. Unfortunately for me, I didn't know how to spell, buy, or use an anemometer, so I irked my dad every time the wind helped me shut my door with a bang.*

you got it (if you foolishly ignored the previous rule).

- Daughters with waist length hair are responsible for unclogging the shower drain by hand (that would be me, and that is enough to make me gag).

- If your hair freezes at night because the house is cold, cut it (unclogging will be easier too).

- And last but not least, never, ever change the thermostat without express written permission from the government (or at the very least, your commanding officer).

-Your father is your commanding officer (SO THE ANSWER WILL BE NO).

Infractions to the above rules were not looked upon favorably and resulted in a variety of groans and throat-clearings, the equivalent of a non-verbal slap on the wrist. Over the years, I received so many of these corrections that I began to categorize them according to sound. Each grunt, sigh, and groan had it's own specific meaning, like a secret code that I finally cracked after putting together all the clues.

For example, Groan #283 meant "here she goes again, that silly little hyena with her out-of-control giggling. Go giggle at someone else's house." Sigh #45 was executed with closed eyes and inferred, "I have no idea what you want. Go ask your mother."

Grades were always a big deal in our house, so a disappointing report card (anything less than all A's) resulted in a deep grunt, followed by a long, drawn-out throat clearing. This was better known as Grunt #53. The grunt translated into "is that the best you could do?"

and the throat clearing meant "do better next time." My all-time favorite non-verbal clue could often be detected when my dad paused momentarily to glance at my messy bedroom floor. Affectionately known as Sheesh #22, it was code for "Your room looks like a pig stye, young lady.* Get in here right now and clean this place up."

By the time I was in my teens my father barely had to speak. Of course, there was the rare occasion when I really screwed up. That's when he dished out the ultimate visual spanking: the dreaded "look." It was more than I could take. I hated to disappoint my father.

Sometimes I would tease him about his repertoire, but my joking was simply a way of disguising the pain I felt at not being able to please him. No matter how hard I tried, the bottom line was always the same: work a little harder and do a little better. Until then, there would be no long talks, no open lap, and no coveted pet name. And no, Alec doesn't count as a pet name when it is *always* preceded by the word Smart.

---

* Rats nests? Pig styes? What were they? Farmers?

Chapter 2

The ~~Big Hairy~~ Barbie Factor

"I think they should have a Barbie with a buzz cut."
Ellen DeGeneres

I did the whole soldier-daughter thing to appease my dad but in my heart, I was anything but a soldier. I was a girly girl who liked to play make-believe with stuffed animals and dolls, though not just any doll would do. I noticed that some of my friends played with dolls that looked like real babies and pretended to be their mommies. That fascination eluded me.

Every Saturday, in between *Scooby Doo* and *Gumby*, I watched commercial after commercial hawking life-like dolls to little girls like me. I was more inclined to beg for Scooby Doo Snacks than a life-like doll. Who wanted a doll that cried, wet, talked, or upchucked (even if it was pretend vomit)? They were far too much work and way too demanding. I got nauseous when my dog threw up, so why would I want a doll that did that? I wanted to play, and that was not play in any way, shape, or form.

Changing make-believe diapers and preparing bottles for fantasy feedings did not sound like fun in the least. It actually seemed like a lot of work, and imaginary work at that, with nothing to show for it. The doll wasn't *really* eating or *really* peeing, so what was the point? I saw it as a contrived marketing scheme designed to make little girls feel like little mothers, and I wasn't buying.

It reminds me of the time-consuming lifeboat drill that cruise lines like Royal Uninhibited make eager-for-fun-passengers do before they set sail. It's a waste of time. In theory, it's a good idea; but no matter how much they practice, when the boat starts to sink, people will still panic, scream for their mothers, and desperately wish they had taken a car trip to Yosemite instead.

The number one reason I wanted any kind of doll was because of her hair. I love hair of all colors, textures, and styles. To this day, when I see a full head of spiraling ringlets, it is all I can do to not reach out and pull the coiling curl down and utter the word "boing!" Some people are even nice enough to let me embrace my inner "boinger," although I typically sneak away fairly quickly just in case they call 911 (something I dis-covered happens far less often if you actually ask permission first).

Yes, I am fascinated by hair (although jewelry comes in a tight second). I never aspired to "do hair" for a living, but I loved to brush and braid, and comb and curl for hours on end.

Perhaps my obsession was genetic. My grandmother had a standing appointment with the "beauty operator" every week. All I could do was envision her head under some sort of space-age gizmo from the Jetsons that magically washed, dried and set her curls. She must have slept sitting up her entire life because I never saw a single blond curl out of place.

Or perhaps it was because an Aunt I barely knew came for a visit once, and she oohed and ahhed over my long blond hair, claiming it looked like "spun gold shimmering in the sun." Me? Shimmering? (Actually, she had me at gold.) Yes, I believe that was the beginning of my love affair with hair. Over the years, I've appreciated the fact that hair doesn't gain weight. It never bloats either. In fact, the thicker it is, the better – something you can't say about waists or thighs. Hair doesn't change depending on the time of the month, and you don't have to swallow enough Midol to de-puff a horse in order to slide on a sparkly headband. Clips and barrettes are one size fits all, and you don't have to hold your breath to fasten them. Yes, I felt special having hair that (at least according to my aunt) looked like spun gold, something only Rumpelstiltskin* knew how to make (even if it did clog the shower drain).

---

* *Rumpelstiltskin was a 19th century Grimm fairy tale about an unusual little fellow who turned straw into gold for a ridiculously high price. He later went on to open his own salon. (I go there.)*

When it came to my dolls and their hair, I made one exception and one exception only. Even then, it was purely for sentimental reasons. The doll's name was Lucy. Lucy was a traditional doll, something I usually avoided, but Lucy was a hand-me-down relic my grandmother pulled out when I came to visit. The emotional tie apparently outweighed having to look at her lackluster locks.

Lucy was part plastic, part cloth with a wadded up bunch of batting inside. She looked like she'd been around the block a few times. She may have been a beauty back in the day, but the years hadn't been kind to poor old Lucy. By the time I got her she needed a lot more than a dolly nip and tuck. She needed a complete overhaul.

Over time, Lucy had become a little creepy looking, like one of those dolls you see in horror films. She was nearly bald, had only a few eyelashes left, and sported one eyelid that didn't fully open. This made her look more like a hung-over stroke victim than a well-loved plaything. I cherished broken-down Lucy, even though most of her hair had fallen out of her large plastic pores. If there was a Hair Club For Dolls, I would have signed Lucy up in a heartbeat.

The year I turned 9, Santa Claus delivered the object of my hair-loving affection: a brand spanking new doll named Velvet. Velvet was the epitome of fabulousness due to her full head of long blond tresses. The coolest thing about Velvet was that her hair length could be changed with a simple push of her plastic belly button. If you decided that long hair was *out* and short hair was *in*, you could make Velvet's style up-to-the-minute any time you wished.*

One day, I decided that long hair was soooo yesterday, and set out to make my Velvet super chic and hip. Instead of coiling up Velvet's hair by turning the little plastic knob on her back to shorten it (like I was *supposed* to), I listened to a creative whim which told me to chop off her blond pony tail with one swift whack of the kitchen scissors. It didn't hit me until an entire *millisecond* after I'd done it, that I had just altered Velvet forever. I gave her an ugly, permanent "in-do." It was the equivalent of pulling up a set of mini blinds and cutting off the cord. Game over. Without a single thought to the final repercussions, I ruined the greatest feature of the doll that I cherished more than anything.

Sadly, my newly shorn Velvet looked more like a deranged psycho than a beauty queen. She was kicked out of the locks-for-love program and relegated to the dolly rehab center, along with poor Alopecia Lucy.

With Velvet out of commission, I turned my attention to the ultra-hip, albeit highly superficial, new

---

* Too bad it isn't that way in real life. That would eliminate the oh-so-painful process everyone refers to as "growing it out." This is the interminable purgatory of hair regrowth endured by every woman who's ever foolishly changed her hairstyle just to be "in."

kid on the block: Barbie. Barbie wasn't just any old doll. She was physically flawless, creatively packaged, and attractively dressed. Barbie came with a built-in boyfriend named Ken and a female cousin named Skipper...both sold separately, of course.

Ken had a built-in six-pack and a perpetual tan like Matthew McConaughey. Unfortunately, Ken's hair resembled a bad toupee, which as you could have guessed, was a deal breaker for me. Skipper had good hair, but was short, flat-footed, *and* flat-chested. With these sub-par attributes, she hardly seemed to fit into this otherwise-perfectly-sculpted family. I always suspected Skipper was adopted though it was never confirmed by Mattel. Either way, the three dolls were an unlikely trio. Barbie was too perfectionistic to ever be caught dead with either one of them in real life.

Barbie had absolutely nothing in common with all the traditional dolls. Unlike realistic dolls, Barbie's sole purpose was to be beautiful. Barbie was the modern ideal of feminine perfection. I never had to worry about doing silly things for Barbie like feeding, burping, or changing her because Barbie never ate. Clearly this was the only explanation for her dazzling measurements of 38-4-38.

Barbie's make-up was always glamorous and expertly applied. The best part about it was that it was permanently painted onto her lovely face, just like her gleaming white smile. She sported perfect pink lips and jet black eyeliner, just like the eyeliner tattoos seared onto high fashion models and well-to-do elderly women who can't see well enough to apply eyeliner themselves any more. Barbie went to bed with make-up on and woke up with make-up on. No acne, no wrinkles, no cold sores. Every man's dream.

Barbie had a plethora of enviable physical traits. Her perpetually manicured hands were in a graceful ballerina position at all times, angled slightly upward at her wrists. This conveniently allowed her to carry a colorful array of designer purses on her forearms, without slippage or carpal tunnel. Barbie also had long, slender fingers that were perpetually free of hangnails, age spots, and that nasty yellow fungus that never goes away.

Barbie's perfect posture highlighted a well-endowed set of eternally perky breasts, which were, presumably, real. (The Special Edition Breast Augmentation Barbie wasn't fully developed yet, due to safety issues. However, safer options were implanted soon after sales of B-cup Barbie began to sag.) Her anti-gravitational chest was undoubtedly her most prominent (and I do mean prominent) feature, especially in contrast to her miniscule 3 mm waist. Clearly, Barbie did not require a liver, spleen or any other vital organs. They simply wouldn't fit.

Finally, Barbie had amazingly perfect feet. She must have been genetically bred to wear stilettos, since her feet only conformed to her collection of plastic high heels. How convenient. (Sales of Orthopedic Footwear Barbie fell in the test market, although miraculously, her arches never did.) Years of wearing nothing but irresponsible footwear would have crippled the average doll, but not Barbie. She was always bunion-free, arthritis-free, and pain-free.

I spent countless hours brushing and styling Barbie's luxurious hair into a shiny, nylon coif. Some girls were lucky enough to get a Special Edition Barbie who came equipped with Quik-Curl hair. Barbie's amazing Quik-Curl hair was moldable, like blond fishing wire impregnated with a thousand dollars' worth of professional styling product. Some days she went curly, some days straight. It was hard to know how to leave Quik-Curl Barbie at the end of the day. It's like the sweet and salty snack dilemma; it's tough to know exactly when to leave well enough alone.

Either way, Barbie's hair never thinned and was always full and bouncy. (Unfortunately for poor Lucy, getting approval for prototype Rogaine Barbie made the FDA pull their hair out, so it got the shaft early on.)

One day I decided Barbie needed real earrings to compliment her coif. Foreshadowing my affinity for poking people with needles, I used a metal straight pin to pierce Barbie's ears. The pin heads conveniently doubled as a shiny pair of silver studs. The earrings looked amazing at first. I was proud as punch of inventing the first DIY Barbie piercing kit. I could even envision myself advertising it on a Saturday morning cartoon commercial. Sadly, after a day or two, Barbie developed a greenish hue around her earlobes, the equivalent of dolly gangrene. Not to worry. Barbie wasn't the average doll; she was perfect. Even a raging staph infection couldn't detract from the exquisite beauty of Barbie's perfectly accessorized plastic head.

Barbie appealed to modern young women for a multitude of reasons. Not only was she a fashionista, she was a real estate mogul as well. She owned a mansion in Malibu, complete with a pool and diving board. In addition, Barbie drove a pink and white convertible, presumably purchased with the paychecks she earned as a doctor, veterinarian, Olympic swimmer, and beauty pageant queen. (Perhaps she sold Mary Kay on the side too, thus the pink car.) Santa never brought me those high dollar Malibu digs, but I was the proud owner of a pink and black Barbie playhouse complete with a tiny clothes rack and miniature clothes hangers. It was adorable, but it smelled strongly of plastic for at least three years. (That couldn't have been good for me.)

Barbie was fun to play with, but as a role model, she lacked perspective. Dolls like Barbie aren't the best example for young girls seeking to develop their selfworth in something other than appearance. Sure, in recent years companies have come out with more "natural" dolls geared toward image conscious young ladies. It's hardly enough, and way overdue. It's a little too late for some of us. Four decades too late.

Perhaps I could write to whoever's in charge of that (hopefully it's not the same inflexible people who handled the time zone debacle) to suggest other, more life-like variations of Barbie. How refreshing it would be to see a more realistic depiction of womanly beauty.

In fact, until we have more real life dolls, such as Acne Barbie and PMS Barbie, I won't be satisfied.

In fact, I can think of dozens of real life versions off the top of my head, such as Cellulite Barbie, or better yet, Bunion Barbie. She comes with two pairs of ugly orthopedic shoes, the Dolly-lama's punishment for years of wearing high heels the size of a skyscraper. Along that same vein, I'd love to see Varicose Barbie. She comes complete with a little purple Sharpie so you can draw on her legs and have matching spider veins. Compression hose sold separately, of course.

For the more "mature audience" (the saggers and draggers of the bunch), it would be nice to have Nip and Tuck Barbie as a realistic rendition of life after 40. She prefers to be called Barbara now, eats dinner at 4:30 pm, and steals pink sweetener packets from restaurants. This vintage edition comes complete with life-like wrinkles and a wide-brimmed hat, something she was too young and stupid to use on the beaches of Malibu. She also comes with a heavy duty night cream, as well as a tub of sunscreen that has an SPF of 200 and is the consistency of cream cheese.

In an ideal world, Nip and Tuck Barbie would come packaged with Plastic Surgeon Ken, whom she met on eDates. (Surgical instruments and gauze available online only.) OK, that may be stretching it a bit, but then again, that's what plastic surgeons do.

No matter. At this point, I'd settle for Menopause Barbie, even if she is a little irritable from time to time. All I ask is that she comes packaged with an oscillating fan and an Uzi. Then, and only then, will I feel like we have really come a long way, baby!

Chapter 3

Reading Between the ~~Wrong~~ Lines

"Reality continues to ruin my life."
Bill Watterson, Calvin and Hobbes

Convinced I could never be the beauty that Barbie was, I turned my attention to what was on the inside of my head rather than on the outside. Brainy girls read a lot, so I made the library a frequent stop.

I loved being at the library, despite the fact that the librarian gave me the heebee jeebees. She had the thickest glasses I'd ever seen on a human being. The reverse magnification made her pupils shrink back into her head like little black pin dots a half mile away. She was short, and had a rather large head making her look more like a giant scary bug than a friendly bookworm.

The worst part was that her super-sized glasses made it impossible to look her straight in the eye. Every time I tried to meet her gaze, she moved her face so she was looking six inches to my right. I had never encountered this phenomenon before. As a military brat, I was expected to *always* look an adult in the eye when speaking to them. (Rule #989. No exceptions.) I was torn.

Each time I approached the check-out desk, I gingerly placed my selections on the counter while I tried in vain to establish direct eye contact with the librarian. Without fail, Bug-Eyed Betty moved her face and stared six inches to my right. So I moved six inches to the right. I moved. She moved. I moved. She moved. Once, I tried using the element of surprise to outsmart her by moving back six inches to the left, double-time, hoping to catch her gaze in the middle. I was unsuccessful. The faster I moved, the faster she moved, snapping her head like a sprinkler with a twitch. Thankfully the desk wasn't round or I would still be there.

Perhaps that's why my favorite books were the ones I borrowed from friends. The most memorable was the ever popular *Are You There God? It's Me, Margaret,* a literary rite of passage for teenage girls. Judy Blume was the go-to author for prepubescent wisdom. Due to the nature of her material, however, I wasn't sure if they were contraband, so I read her works on the down low and always acted like I understood what she was talking about (even though I rarely did).

Who *was* this Judy Blume person, I wondered? (I would have Googled her, but Al hadn't invented the Internet yet.) It was like she knew the questions I wanted to ask even before I knew what they were. She was far too intuitive and straightforward about taboo issues to be anyone's real-life mother, I decided. She could have been an older sister-type, but was too emotionally mature and knew way too much about grown-up issues to be a kid. I was confused because I'd never heard an adult speak so frankly about such personal topics as menstruation and body image before.

My mom never talked about stuff like that except for the occasional reference to "bosoms" here and there. So I was more than a little unnerved when "Aunt Flow" came to visit for the first time a few months before I turned eleven. I tried desperately to manage the situation on my own out of self-consciousness, or ignorance, or both. I even went so far as to look up the word menstruation in the Encyclopedia Brittanica (our version of Google) to see if it would tell me what to do, but alas, it did not. I even whispered, "Are You There God? It's Me, Sally," assuming that's how Margaret figured it out. No response.

Finally, I called my mother at a dinner party to ask her what to do, making her *promise* not to tell my dad, who I was convinced had no idea what a period was in the first place. So you can imagine my feelings of betrayal, as well as utter mortification, the next morning when my father calmly sauntered into my room and said, "So, I hear you're a woman now." I wanted to die.

In addition to Ms. Blume's books, I spent endless

hours reading Nancy Drew mysteries.   After consuming the entire series of mysteries, I happened to noticed that each book had approximately the same number of pages (give or take 5) regardless of the storyline or plot. That didn't seem possible to me. But none of my library reading buddies ever mentioned it, so I wondered if I was the only one who noticed. On the other hand, maybe they did, but nobody wanted to be the one to blow the whistle on the author of such a beloved childhood series. This made me question what was wrong with *me* that I would even consider it. The fact that anyone could write so many stories with practically the same number of pages was a mystery all right. However, that was nothing in comparison to the biggest plot twist of them all. (Spoiler alert.) Author Carolyn Keene was actually a man.   That was a truly mind-blowing twist for a tween girl. It took me years to get over that.

   With all due respect to Nancy Drew and her CSI gal-pals George and Bess, I enjoyed a totally different kind of mystery even more. I could never get enough of the real life mysteries penned by Laura Ingalls Wilder (who was, thankfully, a woman like I thought) in her *Little House on the Prairie* books.

   I didn't know why, but Laura's journey was a mysterious one to me, defined by simple countrified living and random life lessons taught at the dinner table. Each installment of the series increased my desire to live in the less complicated days of gingham dresses and cozy family suppers by the fire. There were no modern conveniences, no television, and no Barbie dolls. Laura wrote fondly of Sundays spent on the front porch, listening to music and talking with her family. She was connected to her family at the deepest core of her being, an integral part of something much larger than herself. It was like being Greek, but with knickers.

Pretending to be Laura, I often rode my bike down the street, imagining that my handlebars were reins, and my bright yellow Schwinn was a trusty steed galloping back to the Little House in the Big Woods where Ma, Pa and poor, blind Mary were waiting for me. The wind rushing through my long golden hair was a blast from the prairie past, blowing away every care in the world like it had for Laura. As I rode, I contemplated what was so inviting about a sparse life in a lean-to and a one-room schoolhouse.

I asked my mother if she too longed for the "good ol' days" when clothing was washed by beating it with sticks in a nearby brook. She muttered something to the effect that washers and dryers were the most fabulous invention since sliced bread and that I would no doubt feel the same when I had my own laundry to do someday (which indeed was the case).

Eventually, my mind wandered to Pa. I often wondered what it would be like to crawl up onto Pa's lap, tight and safe in his arms. Laura and I both had mothers that were sweet and kind, though mine demonstrated that she never really appreciated the Ingalls lifestyle as much as I did. She vehemently refused when I asked if I could call her "Ma." Either way, that never stopped me from hoping that one day I would feel like Laura, an unmistakable daddy's girl with a special pet name all my own.

As time went on, I read anything I could get my hands on, especially if it had an inviting cover or a cute boy on it. Occasionally, I would snag a *Hormone Herald* or *Boy Crazy Monthly* from a friend whose mother regularly bought *The National Enquirer* and believed it to be true.

Teenybopper romance novels caught my eye too, but they were bland reading, at least compared to today's highly sexed teen literature. My books were about average adolescents who were thrilled to go to a school dance with a good-looking boy and swap a little spit.

These days, it's cool to fall in love with hunky heroic vampires who have extraordinary skills and out-of-this-world hair. I'm not really sure when vampires became warm and fuzzy, but it seemed to happen in an instant with little to no warning. Perhaps I was too busy unclogging the shower drain or brushing my hair to notice.

When I was growing up, vampires were brooding *"I-vant-to-suck-your-blood"* types that never went to high school and lurked around in the Dark Shadows. At night, they flew around like bats, going "poof" when exposed to a single ray of sunlight. Boy, have things changed.

I thought Count Chocula was the only "good vampire," but these days nothing could be further from the truth, at least if you are one of those impression-able people who believe everything they see in the movies. I'm not sure who is responsible for the new and improved Vampire 2.0, but those ding-bats are determined to elevate vampires from nefarious blood-suckers to kind, philanthropic do-gooders who utilize their blood banks like a nocturnal Red Cross. In fact, they are more humanitarian than most humans.

Unlike Dracula, these magical creatures don't vanish in the light. Rather, they sparkle like diamonds in the sun. A definite upgrade. Like I said, I don't know where I was when the vampire revolution occurred, but who can argue with progress like that?

In my day, it was attractive for men to be both mortal and tan. Toothy Donnie Osmond and the uber-popular David Cassidy were my top two heartthrobs, followed closely by the adorable Bobby Sherman. I loved Bobby too, but he held a distant third place in my heart, which I credited to the short life of his TV series and his so-so hair. Plus, he wasn't a great singer, a feature on par with great hair. I loved Andy Williams too, with his pale blue eyes and soft tenor voice, but he was a little old for me. (He was born in 1927.)

I always gravitated toward squeaky-clean hunks that could sing. Donnie's blindingly white grin and vocal rendition of "Puppy Love" made me swoon. I listened to that record over and over until the 45 wore thin. (Yes, a 45. It's a record, not a gun. Ask your mother.)

Donnie's closest competitor for my heart (and my hand in marriage, naturally) was David Cassidy, whose thick shag haircut and sly out-of-the-corner-of-his-mouth grin melted my heart every time he sang "I Think I Love You." I smiled every time I heard that song, as though he was personally serenading me from inside the transistor radio (ask your dad about that one).

One day, when my dad was out of town, I made the risky decision to transform the inside of my closet into a shrine for the hunks that were closest to my teeny bopper heart. In what could be called my greatest display of childhood rebellion, I clipped dozens of dreamy pictures of my favorite dreamboats from the glossy Teen magazines and taped them (whaaaat?) to the back of my closet. I knew it was dangerous, but I also knew exactly where to part my hung-up clothing so as to catch a glimpse of Donny, David, and his less attractive but still coo-worthy younger brother Shawn without anyone seeing.

I had to be extremely careful. I would have been in *big trouble* if my father ever found out that I'd adhered a photo directly to a painted surface with (gasp!) Scotch tape. Taping required wall touching, both of which were blatant and punishable violations of the responsible home ownership code. (Refer back to Chapter One if you've already forgotten the rules. I never will.) The whole nefarious endeavor was about as close to being a "wild child" as I ever got. It was thrilling because it was my own personal secret, and needed to remain that way until I went to college or jail, whichever came first.

In the end, I may never have been a traditional "daddy's girl" but my father was always proud of the fact that I could get ready in a flash, follow rules, and decorate my walls without the use of adhesives (at least as far as he knew). That may not be the best trade-off in the world, but hey, there's no point in whining about it now.

Chapter 4

The ~~Not So~~ Friendly Skies

*"Everything is funny
as long as it is happening to somebody else."*
Will Rogers

I freely admit it: I am one of the most directionally challenged individuals on the planet. People claim that a sense of direction is like the ability to spell - either you have it or you don't. Fortunately, I can spell like a champ. Unfortunately, I would get irretrievably* lost on the way to the spelling bee.

The fact that my "gyro is catawampus" (which is my always-polite mother's way of saying I can't find my way out of a paper bag) is a constant source of frustration. I don't know how but I fell through the largest educational fault line possible when it came to geography. The whole

---

Irretrievably. Can I have a definition please? Irretrievably: impossible to regain or recover from the pathetic genetic inability to read a stupid map. Oh, now I get it. I-R-R-E-T-R-I-E-V-A-B-L-Y. Irretrievably.

north-south-east-west thing just never stuck. I can't help but refer to north as "going up" and east as "going right." No matter how hard I try, my brain cannot turn a flat map into a three-dimensional schematic. Thanks to my new best friend Garmin, I know where I am going for the most part, but I spent almost four decades lost and alone before she came "across the pond" to offer assistance (I programmed mine to speak to me in a pleasant British accent).

Suffice it to say, I've stopped to ask for directions more times than Lance Armstrong has doped up. As if I don't feel stupid enough already, when I stop someone and frantically beg for directions, nothing irks me more than hearing them say, "Well, you go north a half a mile, then head east for about 400 yards before heading southwest, blah blah blah." (This is especially exasperating when I've circled the driveway crying for an hour.) It never ceases to amaze me that the Magellans of the world haven't realized that if someone asks for directions in a high pitched voice, with shallow respirations and a thready pulse, they are not going to wrap their head around directions given in terms of latitude and longitude.

While I have appreciated all the help over the years, here's a scoop for you would-be geography teachers; if I am so lost that I have to pull over and ask a complete stranger for directions, I don't need a tutorial on land navigation. What I *really* need is a police escort. That's how lost I am. At the very least, I need specific instructions including pertinent and recognizable landmarks such as "go left at the Taco Bell or turn right after the Dunkin Donuts" and so forth. For goodness sakes, people, speak in terms I can understand.

As embarrassing as it is, there is a predictable trajectory to my behavior when I am lost, even if I am using a GPS. (Hey, lost is lost, even if I do have Mary Poppins in the car trying to help me.) If I remotely suspect I am headed the wrong way, my pulse begins to quicken. If I can't confirm within a few seconds that I am on the correct path, I become agitated and insecure. If I *know* I am going the wrong way, things get ugly, and I start to unravel. If I am dead certain that I am going the wrong way and it's dark outside, I become completely unglued.

Finally, the worst possible scenario is being lost, in the dark, *and late*. This is the ultimate triumvirate of terror. It sends me into orbit and reduces my otherwise competent self into someone barely recognizable. At this point, my inner compass is spinning out of control like the altimeter on an airplane crashing at sea. In these instances, eyewitnesses have supposedly reported violent bouts of paranoia and cold sweats, leading to the irrational crossing of medians and exit ramps in my minivan (the suburban definition of off-roading), or so I've heard.

The sad thing is, I have absolutely no idea why I do this. Sometimes I wonder if I was abandoned at night on the side of the road as a small child. Of course, that's completely ridiculous and out of the question, but there has to be a rational explanation for the irrational chain reaction that occurs when I'm lost. Too bad George W. Bush wasn't in charge when I was in school. It's painfully obvious that I was the child left behind. I've never found my way back since.

Highway lingo is ridiculously complex to me, and hard to remember. Instructions like "circle around the beltway until you get to the bypass" sound more like stomach stapling instructions than directions to a party. In contrast to road jargon, I found it easier to navigate the United States by memorizing simple three letter airport codes, using the map conveniently found in the seat back pocket directly in front of me.

My dad flew for a commercial airline, so thankfully most of my childhood travel was via the Friendly Skies. Unlike the general population, I feel more comfortable in a plane than a car, knowing that the pilot has a better sense of direction than I do. (Then again, who doesn't?) I also like that I can get up and go to the bathroom anytime I want and still be barreling forward at high speed, something that cannot be said about car travel. The autopilot feature is a plus, but that is technically cheating. (Even *I* could do *that*. You can't call yourself an expert at directions when the plane is driving itself.) Piloting a plane would be easy compared to driving. At 30,000 feet there are no sudden turns, no gravel roads, and no pedestrians to hit. On the other hand, you can't roll down the window and ask for directions at that altitude.

I love air travel because I learned at an early age how to navigate my way through it. In the airline world, directions are given in terms of cities*, not interstates, using easy to understand airport codes instead of confusing zip codes. Most of the codes make sense and give you a hint as to which city the airport is located in. For example, LAX is Los Angeles, and CLT is Charlotte, and so forth. I flew out of Chicago for the most part, which by all sensibility should have the code CHI or CGO. But that would make too much sense. Chicago is ORD because they built O'Hare Airport in the middle of an old abandoned **OR**char**D**. Sure. Everybody makes *that* jump.

Flying used to be a lot of fun. Before the events of September 11th, security was minimal at best. Back then, it wasn't uncommon to arrive at the airport five minutes before takeoff and jump onto the plane like a flying squirrel as it began to push back from the accordion-like walkway.

In those days, the biggest threat to air safety was the possibility of being hijacked to Cuba, and the horrific meals coach passengers were expected to choke down. (Air sickness bags aren't just for the air.)

The only safety precautions employed at that time were an x-ray machine for luggage and large, clearly posted signs banning any sort of bomb references. At the bottom of the sign it read:

---

* It wasn't until college that I realized Vermont was not a city, but an actual state large enough to support an international airport. Like I said, the whole geography thing really never stuck.

ALL COMMENTS WILL BE TAKEN SERIOUSLY.
NO JOKING ALLOWED.

Like most kids, I assumed jokes were a *good* thing. People smiled. Ha Ha. People laughed. Ha Ha. The folks who made the sign must have been kidding. Funny one-liners kept popping into my head, but I repeatedly pushed them back down into my brain like a mental game of whack-a-mole, just in case the signs were serious.

*"We're going to have a **blast** on this trip!" Haha…*

*"Sorry my suitcase is a mess, Mom. A **bomb** must have gone off in there!" Hehe…*

*"Don't **blow up** at me, but I forgot my swimsuit!" Hardy har har…*

On and on it went inside my mind, but I knew better than to say anything, lest I get the dreaded "look."

These days, air travel requires a two-day head start to accommodate the TSA with its bomb-sniffing-foot-odor-whiffing-pants-unzipping protocol. Even simple hygiene products designed to keep you from smelling like a traveling sewer can cause a serious delay if they are not contained in the right size Ziploc baggie.

Seriously? Even if I had the scholastic where-withal to combine 3 oz. of baby shampoo, lip gloss, and a can of hairspray to make an explosive, I seriously doubt a plastic baggie would contain the blast. If I were smart enough to do *that*, I'd brag about it to everyone waiting in the security line even if it landed me in jail faster than you can say "passport."

As a kid, flying was a real adventure and not just because we were on vacation. My family never flew the "normal" way, with reservations and tickets and such. As airline employees, we flew "stand-by."

Stand-by passengers are often referred to as "non-revs," a term which stands for non-revenue-generating-seat-fillers-the-airline-loses-money-on-so-the-employees-don't-have-to-treat-you-as-if-their-jobs-depended-on-it-like-they-do-for-people-who-are-paying-real-money-to-fly. (Believe it or not, that's the short version.) In other words, non-revs merited the same status as unwanted kittens, and were greeted at the gate with the same warm welcome Mary got at the Inn.

All non-revs are required by the airline to dress formally. Denim was forbidden in any way, shape or form. This really irked me. Hour after miserable hour, I waited for a seat, fidgeting in my control-top panty hose and overly starched blouse, while paying passengers casually sauntered into First Class wearing nothing but a swimsuit and thongs.*

Back in the day, flip-flops were commonly referred to as thongs, a fun version of cheap summer footwear. This is not to be confused with the completely unfun cheap-looking-devil-bred-crack-flossing-thread-of material undoubtedly designed by men to torture women who then think of nothing else on a minute-to-minute basis but how to alleviate the unrelenting discomfort that comes from wearing a thong. There, Victoria. The Secret's out. I hope you're happy.

Of course, I knew better than to whine about it. Instead, I silently vowed that one day I would purchase a full fare ticket to Hawaii and fly there wearing nothing but comfy shorts and a tube top. I'm still waiting for that day, but it had better happen soon or the tube top will be resting on top of the flip flops.

As early as I can remember, we had been sternly schooled on how to behave at the airport. "Flying is a privilege," my father reminded us before every trip, with his uncanny ability to give us "the look" and "the lecture" at the same time. (That must have taken some practice in the mirror.)

He was never more serious about our behavior than at the airport. As a pilot, the airport was *his* domain, and as such, a pilots' family must be on their best behavior at all times. He had an entirely separate set of rules for airport protocol, all of which needed to be enacted in addition to the lengthy set of home rules. (Luckily for me, I have a good memory.) My father stringently warned us that if we did not follow the rules, it could cost him his job (not to mention embarrass El Capitan), and we would lose our flying privileges forever. (There goes Hawaii.)

We were to wait patiently, smile graciously, and act as though we would be thrilled to death if the gate agent let us on the plane, even if that meant we were strapped on top of the wing with bungee cords.

We weren't to so much as flinch if they asked

us to flap our arms during flight or plunge our feet to the ground to help land the plane like Barney Rubble. We were to smile, nod our heads yes, and staunchly maintain the no-whining mandate. Non-rev flying rules were clear: ask for nothing, bother no one, never talk to the flight attendant unless they talk to you first and if they did, the yes and no answer format applied just like at home. We were to avoid looking hungry and only take food if every other paying passenger in the Friendly Skies had their fill of sustenance and insisted upon giving their leftovers to the poor starving children with NON-REV stamped across their foreheads. And finally, even if we were dying of oxygen deprivation, we were *never ever* to ring the call bell for service. I felt so privileged.

That's how we had to act when we were lucky enough to get ON the plane. Sometimes they didn't even let us on. This is called being "bumped," which made me wonder if a fat old lady got a kick out of knocking us down the plane stairs, laughing at us while she placed her enormous backside in our seats. Getting bumped forced us to wait around for the next available open seat, which could be a few hours or a few days after. We never knew.

The only certainty in flying stand-by was the extra time on our hands for airport exploration and "people-watching" as my mother called it. She did the people watching while I did the exploring. A favorite time-passer was to check the pay phones (again, go ask your mother) for left-behind quarters or dimes. Every once in a while, I found a stray coin in the dirty silver change drop and celebrated my winnings as if I'd just won the lottery.

Airport restrooms provide the most unusual source of entertainment. It's hard to believe now, but the bathroom stalls in ORD used to require a dime to open the door. It was a pay-to-pee-policy, if you will, and very unaccommodating to the flying female. I watched with great amusement as dime-less women checked every door for an entrance into immediate relief after a long flight. Some ladies even checked to see if the small space under the door was passable. The money-grubbing airport had already thought about that possibility, making the distance from the floor to the door so tight that a skinny limbo champion couldn't shimmy underneath, much less a normal sized woman with a full bladder. I decided that in the future I would carry a spare dime in my purse at all times, or at the very least, avoid liquids if passing through O'Hare.

As a frequent flyer, I was good at entertaining myself on the plane, often by imagining that David Cassidy would be waiting for me at our destination. I always brought along a book too, usually a Nancy Drew mystery, in spite of my same-page-outrage.

This time, however, I pulled out something

very different to read; a large print Bible. I borrowed it from the church basement where the senior citizens met for Sunday school. It's not every day you see an 8-year-old embark on in-flight reading from a huge Bible, so I'm sure I got more than my share of who's-the-weird-kid stares but I didn't notice. I was just happy that all the books in the Bible were not the exact same number of pages, a refreshing change from you-know-who.

Starting with Genesis, I skimmed over the begets and begots, the boring stuff people associate with the Bible. However, not far into the Old Testament I came upon a passage concerning the Jewish custom of circumcision. The passage used a certain term regarding male anatomy with which I was unfamiliar. I considered asking the flight attendant just this once but thought better of it.

Not knowing what the questionable term meant, I decided to ask my mother, who was sitting three rows in front of me due to our non-revs-sit-where-we-tell-them-to arrangement. In order to get my mother's full attention, I called her name out loudly, so she could hear me over the roar of the engines and the chatter of the other passengers. She leaned her head out into the aisle and looked back over the seats just in time for me to shout, "Hey Mom....what's a pen-is?" (My mispronunciation made it rhyme with tennis.) My mother's facial expression confirmed one of two things: a) she herself did not know the answer to the question, or b) I should never ask something of that nature again, especially in public.

It seemed like a simple question, but apparently, it was not. I never got an answer. My mother refused, I was confused, and I'm sure the other passengers were more than amused.

Chapter 5

The Red Cross
~~Your Fingers~~ Babysitter

"Some people have no idea what they're doing,
and a lot of them are really good at it."
George Carlin

My father is a firm believer in self-sufficiency and hard work, both very admirable traits. In search of the key to my father's heart, I wanted to embody those traits too, even though I was a kid and didn't fully understand what it meant to be self-sufficient. I had no idea what bootstraps were, but I knew without a doubt that I was to pull myself up by them should the need arise.

It soon became apparent that self-sufficiency involved money, of which I had none. The ability to support yourself financially rather than relying on any one else, especially the government (a novel idea these days), was the ultimate goal in becoming a responsible adult. I wanted more than anything for my dad to be proud of me, so I set out to be self-sufficient as soon as I could. Unfortunately, this involved finding a way to make money.

I didn't have any marketable skills, but as "they" say, "where there's a *will* there's a *way*," a frequent adage for bootstrap puller-uppers. I had a will when it came to being independent, so I found a way to secure a few odd jobs. Self-sufficiency: here I come.

One of those jobs was pet-sitting for my neighbors while they were out of town. I loved that job for three simple reasons:

Pay

After all, that was the point.

Popsicles.

These particular neighbors always had a gigantic supply of freeze pops in a variety of unnatural colors, something my mother refused to buy. They were the kind in those long plastic tubes that are impossible to open without getting little bits of plastic stuck in your mouth that you have to spew out like a watermelon seed. The blue ones were my favorite.*

The neighbor lady said I could have a freeze pop every time I let the dog out. After two or

---

* I could never tell what flavor the blue pops were supposed to be, but they definitely didn't taste like blueberries. I racked my brain all summer long trying to figure out what other foods were naturally blue, but I came up empty. Oh well. It never stopped me from eating the whole box.

three blue freeze-sicles, my lips turned purple like a zombie, which I thought was funny, albeit ugly. Needless to say, I went over there so frequently the other neighbors probably thought the poor pooch had a bladder infection. (Either that, or I was a lonely kid with poor circulation.)

Performing

Finally, the best thing about this job (besides the cash) occurred nightly, during my final piddle-now-or-forever hold-your-pee run of the day.

Perched on the back of the house was a super bright floodlight. I routinely turned it on to help Fido mark his spot. With one dramatic flip of a switch, the neighbor's back yard became my own personal theatre. The patio was now my stage, and the spotlight beckoned.

That summer the movie *Grease* came out, and I saw it four times in the first week. Sure, John Travolta had great hair and could sing, but I was more enamored with the silky smooth voice of Olivia Newton-John. I wanted to sing like her in the worst way.

So night after night, with no one watching (and the kind of freedom you only feel when singing into a hairbrush), I belted out "Summer Nights" to a sold-out crowd of crickets and grasshoppers. There, in the glow of a simple floodlight, I *became* Olivia Newton-John, in all her blond-haired, spectacular soprano glory.

From that summer on, I was hooked on singing (which is similar to being Hooked on Phonics, but with a melody).

Singing led me to my favorite source of income on this road to self-sufficiency: babysitting. My high school show choir director had two small children, so he was regularly in need of sitters. He asked me if I had any babysitting experience to which I automatically answered, "Yes Sir! I love to babysit!" Instinctively, I executed the proper military response, but thankfully was able to stop myself from going into a full salute.

I may have been genuinely enthusiastic about the opportunity to earn some cash (thus furthering my journey to self-sufficiency), but to say I loved to babysit was a bit of a stretch. My expertise with children was, let's just say, a work in progress. I had logged my fair share of babysitting hours, but I wouldn't say I was even remotely good at it, much less loved it. I wasn't particularly fond of kids in general, especially the whiney ones. Some girls are naturally great babysitters, with a built-in affinity for children. I wasn't one of them. Compared to them, I would classify myself as more of a so-so babysitter with a few hidden agendas.

As far as credentials went, I was very "official" *looking*. Like all good sitters, I had completed the see-how-responsible-I-am babysitting class offered by the Red Cross at our local hospital.

Here are the two most important take-aways I gleaned from this four-week course:

1) The Heimlich maneuver should never be used on a choking victim if they can audibly speak or cough.

2) At the first sign of fire, immediately remove all children from the burning building and call 911 while you usher them to the end of the driveway and wait for help.

That's it. That's all I heard.

I can't remember anything after that because while the instructor was yammering on and on about all the *other* vitally important safety tips a sitter needs to know, I could only think of one thing. "Hasn't it ever occurred to anyone that small children standing at the end of a driveway have a high probability of getting run over by large, incoming fire trucks? I thought the point was to keep the children safe, but here they are telling us to put them directly in harm's way. How come I'm twelve and I am the only one who sees this discrepancy?" Surely I wasn't the first person to notice the hypocrisy in their "logic".

When all was said and done, I decided to keep mum just like I did with Nancy Drew and The Mystery of the Same Page Outrage. I wasn't about to risk losing my newly laminated card by blowing the whistle on the Red Cross. How else was I going to prove to parents that I was genuinely qualified to sit on their babies?

Graduating from the course didn't automatically transform me into a childcare expert. In fact, all it meant was that I was now in possession of a cool laminated card, identifying me as a certified Red Cross babysitter.

It also meant that I could justify charging real money for my services, which was the primary reason I wanted to babysit in the first place. (Independence, here I come!) The truth was, I didn't really *like* babies. I merely liked the money that babysitting generated, and "sitting" was all I hoped it would entail.

In the beginning, the mothers who hired me must have sensed my lack of childcare expertise. I suspected this because most of my early sitting jobs did not include feeding or bathing children, which, by the way, seemed like a total waste of a Heimlich-trained sitter. How could I perfect my anti-choking maneuvers if I never had the chance to use them? Feeding a kid was the only way I saw to get in some much-needed practice.

The no-bathing part, on the other hand, was a smart move on the mother's part. Quite frankly, giving children a bath made me nervous. Even though our instructors taught us about the dangers of leaving children unattended in the tub, I had not racked up enough hands-on experience in that department to be left alone with a real, living child. Of course, I knew that bathing without supervision can lead to drowning. (I really got my money's worth out of the course). However, the rescue protocol was still a bit hazy. I couldn't remember whether I should pat a drowning victim on their back or shove a choking child's head under water. Either way, I was grateful not to be put in that decision-making position without more real life field time experience. Thankfully, smart mothers knew better than to expect too much from an adolescent newbie, even if she *was* an official card-carrying Red Cross graduate.

Naps and bedtime were a totally different story. That was my favorite part of the whole gig, as it embodied the "sitting" I had naively envisioned. Finally, peace and quiet. I was grateful that most of the children I sat for had to take a nap or be "put down"* for the night during my watch.

I was not a huge fan of children, but *sleeping* children were a different story. They were motionless, quiet, and downright easy money. A child in deep slumber meant they were snug in their beds and safe from harm (or me) unless the house was on fire, in which case I had been specifically told to evacuate them from their beds into the dangerous path of a large emergency vehicle. I will point out here that dragging an infant out of their crib is in direct conflict to the universal adage that you never wake a sleeping baby.

All of this caused me to wonder how mothers keep all these conflicting mandates straight. Are all these rules in addition to the household rules, or do some of those get to slip by the wayside once you become a parent? My head was spinning with all the do's and don'ts of being responsible for children, and I was only there for a few hours. I wondered what type of course a woman is required to take before having a child of her own. (Surprisingly, the only requirements for becoming a mother are a uterus and a pulse, and I

---

*I had only heard the term "put down" in regards to animals. So you can understand how shocked I was the first time I heard a parent use this term in regards to a child. I was afraid to watch.

doubt they give away laminated cards just for having those.)

Unfortunately, there is one universal prerequisite for every babysitter who is asked to care for a non-potty-trained child, and that is to master the art of the diaper. That was the worst part of the whole babysitting process.

Some moms at that time were hip and progressive, using new-fangled disposable diapers.* I loved disposable diapers. The tape was easy to slap on and didn't cause a trip to the emergency room if you "missed" while wrangling a moving target. Even though the occasional misplaced piece of adhesive tape left a little red mark on Sleepy Head's Michelin-tire-thigh, the leaky parts were covered and the bed stayed dry. Everyone was happy.

On the other hand, cloth diapers were my nemesis, the bedtime dragon I was too inexperienced to slay. As a childcare amateur, I couldn't see the point of using cloth diapers versus disposable. I began to believe that cloth diapers were used by women with an apparent lack of anything better to do than bleach and fold countless white rectangles of cotton. I hated cloth diapers because they were extremely difficult to secure on a wriggling infant without causing puncture wounds or torn ligaments. In my mind, they were an

---

If you were born any time within the last century, the evolution of diapers within my lifetime is equivalent to the evolution of transportation for my grandmother who saw the horse and buggy replaced by space travel. Diapers have come a long way. Within your lifetime, you will probably witness the genetic alteration of DNA making it possible for a newborn to forgo diapers altogether. Lucky you.

unnecessary evil (for both of us) once disposable diapers were readily available. The fear in my eyes when being shown a changing table stacked with cloth diapers should have let those particular mothers know that they were going to need an emergency stash of disposables on hand for when I visited.

One such cloth-loving mother didn't get the hint. She requested that I double diaper her precious little Snook-ems before naptime. I gave it my best try, really I did, but between the folding, pinning, squirming and sobbing (me, not the baby), I gave up. By the time I was done swaddling that baby, he looked like his legs had been poked through a gigantic marshmallow, making it impossible for him to lie flat in the crib.

Despite my best efforts, I decided that cloth diapers were an unfair imposition in exchange for minimum wage, so my babysitting mantra became "let 'em sop 'til they drop."

There was a reward to all that wrangling however, and it only happened when the last little crib-rat drifted off to Snooze-land with a dry dipe-ee and a pass-ee in place. (The mommy slang had started to rub off on me.) That's when I began the best part of the whole babysitting process: the pantry raid.

Sweets were taboo in my house, so babysitting doubled as both a money maker and a tasty forbidden-sugar-free-for-all. As soon as I could hear the rhythmic breathing of my sacked-out charges, I crept down the hall like an ant to the picnic.

I was amazed at how many cabinets across Chicagoland were filled with the forbidden fruit of sugary treats. There were cookies, puddings, pretzels, and cakes, most of which I didn't recognize. Countless freezers were loaded with fruit-flavored, double-wide popsicles, the kind you snap in half with your thumbs (although they *never* come out even). Popsicles and pretzels were ok, but I was never truly happy until I found what I was really craving: chocolate.

With the speed and accuracy of a highly train-ed Marine, I hunted down my edible targets in a stealthy manner. Once I safely acquired "the package," I snarfed its contents down with reckless abandon. I consumed countless coco-bakes, chocolate custard pies, yellow sponge tubes, and the occasional leftover Halloween candy with abandon. There were a few houses that stocked up on fruit and raisins, but I steered clear of those jobs in favor of sitting for folks who spent plenty of money in the junk food aisle.

As luck would have it, I discovered the Fort Knox of snack stashes completely by accident when I covered for a fellow Red Cross trainee at the last minute. I thought I was doing *her* a favor, when in fact *I* was the true beneficiary of the deal. I could hardly contain my excitement when I came across a freezer full of famous baker snack cakes*, the kind with white creamy filling and shiny chocolate frosting. I had hit the mother lode, the sitter's jackpot.

---

* *It wasn't until I took American history that I realized Dolly Madison was a historical figure and not a famous baker. I guess geography wasn't the only academic crack I fell through.*

The fact that the snacks were frozen didn't deter me in the least. My best friend had shown me how to eat frozen chocolate chip cookies by thawing one bite at a time with hot exhaled air (a valuable life tip). To my delight, the technique worked equally well on cupcakes.

Of course, smart babysitters never want their employers to know how much snacking has transpired, lest they look inattentive or irresponsible. After all, parents are paying you to sit, not to snack. Therefore, every good sitter should be familiar with the following rules to successful but stealthy snacking on the job.

~ Never leave wrappers out as evidence.

This should be self-explanatory. A complete and thorough cleanup of the kitchen is a must to eliminate all suspicion that you have actually cost the family double in sitting fees when consumed snacks are taken into account.

~ Never open a new box of anything.

Too obvious. People always remember opening a box of something delicious. If it wasn't them, they wonder *who* opened it and why they weren't privy to the goods right off the bat. I don't know why it works this way, it just does.

~ Never eat the last item in the box.

Again, way too obvious, and dangerous. A lot of folks look forward to enjoying the last treat in the box and savor it because either, a) they can't mentally stomach the fact that they ate the whole thing, especially in one sitting, or b) they are hiding it from someone else who might eat it before they do. Either way, the final morsel had better be there when they come looking for it or foul play will be suspected. They might even begin blaming innocent family members who happened to witness the raid when you thought they were safe in bed. Trust me, if you back a small child into a corner about missing snacks, they'll give you up in a heartbeat.

In the unfortunate event that you forget this rule and accidentally eat the last bite, you must:

~ Cover your tracks carefully by removing ALL incriminating evidence.

This can be done in one of two ways:

a) by hiding the telltale empty container in your purse to be disposed of at a later date (heads up, bring a roomy tote to all future babysitting jobs) or

b) by placing the garbage in the homeowner's trash, but only by tucking it underneath other trash so it's undetectable to the naked eye. Tying up the small trash bag and dumping it into the big trash (usually located in the garage or outside) adds an extra layer of security. No parent returning from a pleasant time out ever rummages through their outside trash cans looking for evidence of sitter snack consumption. They are simply too tired or in too good a mood after being released from their parental responsibilities for a bit. Besides, a clean counter and a fresh liner in the trash can makes you look extra tidy. This is a tip-worthy trait providing extra money as well as safe-snacking in one fell swoop.

Last, but not least…

~ Always finish snacking a minimum of thirty minutes before the estimated time of parental return.

This critical step provides an adequate cushion of time needed to accomplish evidence containment, as well as facilitate the removal of stray facial crumbs and chocolaty tooth slime. Ignoring this rule can be disastrous. I say this from first hand experience because I once got cocky and ignored my own set of ironclad rules. Fifteen minutes before the parental ETA, I unwrapped a neon green Popsicle and began to enjoy it with my feet up on the sofa (something I could only do at other people's houses, as it was against our homeowner rules). As a babysitting professional, I should have known better. I may not have been an expert at sitting by this time, but I did consider myself to be quite the professional snacker.

As luck would have it, I heard the garage door open mid-lick and I panicked. My brain froze. Not with the standard cold-food-ingestion brain freeze, but with an even more painful uh-oh-I-don't-want-to-be-caught-with-this-popsicle-in-my-hand brain freeze. In a moment of complete stupidity and utter self-protection, I stuffed the half-eaten lime-flavored Popsicle under the sofa cushion I was sitting on, which was, regrettably, white. I held my breath for the next few days waiting for a call complaining to my mother about the incident. After about a month, I assumed the family must have moved since I never heard from them again.

All in all, I credited myself with a fair job of babysitting resulting in a net score of zero child-related deaths and one possibly-ruined sofa. The only real blemish on my babysitting record involved a family whose four young children allegedly drank apple juice the whole time I was there, giving them diarrhea all night, or so the mom said. I never actually saw it happen because I was on the phone dealing with a boyfriend break-up.

I may not have been a babysitting expert, but I continued to get plenty of work. This proved to me that indeed, where there's a will, there is a way. It also told me that expert or not, I provided a very valuable service to the frazzled moms and dads of Chicagoland who desperately needed fire safety assurance from a snack-scarfing-card-carrying-Red-Cross-approved babysitter.

Chapter 6

College is Full of
~~Misleading~~ Information

*"I have never let my schooling interfere
with my education."*
Mark Twain

I always knew I'd go to college. Whether I was
going to be a neurosurgeon or a graffiti artist, college
was a household expectation, a foregone conclusion,
an educational given. Higher learning was my ticket
to responsibility and self-sufficiency, or so I was told.
My parents routinely proclaimed that a solid education
would allow me to accomplish anything I set my mind
to, except, perhaps, become President of the United
States because of the whole born-in-Japan thing. Thankfully, I am not drawn to politics in the least, so that
was never a crushing blow.

My grandmother's generation rarely went to
college. Women of that era were expected to stay
home and keep house. They made dinner and babies

like clockwork. By the time I went to college, women were considered academic equals, encouraged to attain credentials other than their MRS degree.

One thing was certain. I was not headed to college to look for a husband. If I were in the market for a husband, I wouldn't have spent countless hours filling out scholarship applications and studying for the ACT. I would have lounged at the pool instead. I could only assume that the girls who were out looking for Mr. Right were probably the same ones who played with burping dolls and babysat for the sheer joy of it. Not my crowd.

All I knew for sure was that college was the next step in my journey toward self-sufficiency. It would cost my parents more than a few bucks but it would be worth it.* It was the intangible dangling carrot at the end of a four-year degree. My plan was to make a good living, and be completely independent as soon as I could. My dad would be so proud.

College appeared to be somewhat of a dichotomy. On one hand, it was a sure road to independence and success (again, so I was told). On the other hand, I was told it could be an environment fraught with a whole new set of dangers and temptations.

Typically, I was taught to ask my dad for money only in an emergency. He then went on to define an emergency as "when your leg gets cut off and you have to buy a new one." Even then, he wanted the change.

I'd heard about "liberal professors," scholastic hippies who could make you so open-minded that your brain leaked out. I'd also been warned about the growing use of drugs and alcohol on campuses across the country. Some colleges were nefariously labeled "party schools." I wasn't sure, but the implication was that I could become an alcoholic against my will on the very first day of class if I unwittingly ended up at one of those schools.

Good looking "college boys" came with their own separate warning label, like an attractively packaged bottle of wine that was better for looking at than for drinking. Sure, they were inviting on the outside, but if you weren't careful, they were capable of wreaking havoc, especially in the decision-making department.

I began to wonder what it was about institutes of higher learning that made guys inherently dangerous. Perhaps crossing the campus perimeter caused some sort of genetic mutation, transforming regular Joes into regular Jerks, especially at "party schools."

If that were true, the mutation was magnified once a guy joined a fraternity. All one had to do was refer to frat house movies to prove that theory. Clearly this mutation causes the exaggerated hormonal antics of crazy coeds, forcing all college males to participate in food fights and alcohol-induced streaking. I braced myself for the possibility that every dorm across America was filled with drunken Charlie Sheen types who hoped and groped for an unsuspecting female not equipped with a can of pepper spray or a Breathalyzer.

In the end it didn't really matter. Even if all of the warnings were true, nothing was going to dampen my enthusiasm for college. I wanted my independence more than anything.

The one consistent piece of advice I got about going away to school was to "Be Careful." This worn-out phrase is about as helpful as the uber-nebulous "have a nice day." Both are well intentioned and spoken out of love and concern, but all they really accomplish is to make the speaker feel better knowing they've said it.

Think about it. The motherly adage "Be careful" is helpful in theory only. Doesn't everyone try to be careful on some level? Do we really need some-one to tell us that? Outwardly, I echoed the politically-correct-good-girl response of "I will!" But on the inside, my inner twin Alec (who is apparently *so smart,* every-one calls her that automatically) had to restrain herself from saying, "Thank you SO MUCH for saying that! Geez, before you reminded me to be careful, I was going to go all crazy and ignore every possible rule of good judgment, possibly incurring injury to myself, or others. But luckily, you came along, and reminded me to be careful. Good thing you're around for that or I would probably be dead by now." (Thankfully, my inner Alec has learned to hold her tongue.)

At this time in my life I would have preferred to be given practical, detailed advice, the kind that can help you avert *real* disaster. Specific instructions such as "always smell clear liquids before you drink them" or "don't trust people who give you headache medicine from an unmarked bottle" are straightforward and are much better examples of helpful advice, especially to college students. Truly valuable input might also include insightful tips like "when your roommate says she is having a friend sleep over, don't assume you're invited," or "boys who say they have chemistry with you are not talking about their class schedule." Those types of direct statements offer real-time practical suggestions that are much more helpful for future coeds than "be careful."

Of course, out of human habit, I still tell people in passing to "have a nice day," rather than something *more specific* like "hope you find a twenty dollar bill on the ground," or "nobody likes a whiner, so keep it positive!" Unfortunately, truly helpful platitudes are *much* harder to think of on the fly.

While I don't profess to be a rocket scientist, my grades were good enough to get me where I wanted to go. Plus, my dad's job with the airline made it possible to fly anywhere in the country for very little money, so I never seriously considered a school within driving distance. That was probably a good idea anyway, considering I might get lost on the way there and miss college altogether.

My best friend and I decided to matriculate together at a private university a thousand miles from home. (Matriculate is a just a fancy word that means to attend an institution of higher learning where people pay a lot of money to learn useless words like matriculate.)

My best friend and I were more like sisters than friends. We met each other in kindergarten, but waited until the age of 8 to declare our BFF status. (What took so long I'll never know.) We had our own private language, like the kind twins use. We didn't have to speak at all if we didn't want to, but when we needed to share a private thought in public we used our secret language, something that annoyed our parents to death.

I couldn't wait to room with my friend. In all the years I'd known her, I never once felt self-conscious, or insecure about my height, weight, ACT score, or anything else for that matter. I loved that I never had to explain a thing to her. We had shared every significant life event up to that point, so it was only natural that we journey towards independence together too. Besides, she made me laugh all the time, and what could be better than that?

Together, we spent hours meticulously (which is different than matriculously...anyone who's matriculated knows that) decorating our dorm room with matching comforters and accessories from Target. We hung up posters of furry little kittens, with inspirational sayings on them like "Seven days without prayer makes one weak." (Awwww.) Hanging things up on the wall at college was completely different from hanging things up at home. In the dorm, no one cared if we used scotch tape, push pins, or crazy glue just as long as we could take it off by the end of the year. No more thermostats, no more drains to unclog, and no more homeowner rules. College was better than I ever imagined.

I declared Nursing as my major from the git-go. I really didn't know what nurses did, but in kindergarten I dressed up as Florence Nightingale for Halloween and helped the teacher put a Band-Aid on a classmate. She said I would make a great nurse, and I guess the thought stuck.

Unfortunately, in *real* nursing school it wasn't about wearing white tights and blue capes. In fact, declaring yourself a nursing major came with a certain set of expectations for which I was completely unprepared. Somehow I must have missed the here's-what-you're-supposed-to-know-if-you-want-to-be-a-nurse memo. I blame my kindergarten teacher.

During my first week in the dorm, a couple of students showed up in our doorway asking what my major was. At first I thought these gals were making a social call, like new students do when they meet their fellow dorm mates at the beginning of the year. Then, one of them rolled up her pant leg and asked me if she could "show me something." I quickly went through my mental file cabinet wondering if this was one of those situations I was supposed to avoid when she said, "I need help with a medical problem and I thought you could help." When I laughed out loud she looked perplexed.

Every other day, the pattern continued. Student after student asked me for medical advice until it finally hit me. Somehow, nursing students were automatically expected to handle every sort of medical situation without ever having had a day of nursing class. Didn't they know I was taking general classes like everyone else at this point? I didn't have the first clue how to handle an emergency, especially a medical one. If they only knew how much trouble I had with the fire truck/driveway dilemma, they would have never asked.

It soon became clear that First Aid for nose-bleeds, scrapes, headaches and sprained ankles were supposed to be easy fixes for me simply because I WANTED to be a nurse. Apparently, all good nursing students have Band-Aids, tourniquets and surgical equipment on hand, as well as the knowledge required to use them.

I found the whole thing to be extremely unfair. I hadn't taken a single hour of basic anatomy or physiology, yet I was expected to diagnose heart attacks, brain tumors, and hepatitis (hepa-who?). I didn't even know where the kidneys were, much less know if there was an infection brewing in them. Apparently these were insignificant details to my pseudo-patients.

The unrealistic expectations associated with "wanting to be a nurse" started to annoy me. It wasn't just unfair, it simply didn't make sense. Flight crews wouldn't scour the aisles during an in-flight emergency looking for a kid with a pair of fake plastic wings pinned to his chest and force him to make an emergency landing, would they? No, of course not. The Secret Service would never drive the President's motorcade over a bridge designed by a first year drafting student, would they? Never. And no finance committee in their right mind would hand over the federal budget to be balanced by a freshman accounting major. On second thought, maybe that's what they *should* do, given the success of those currently in charge of reducing the deficit.

(Better yet, let's give some 5th graders a shot. What could it hurt?) Needless to say, I was more than a little miffed at the way nursing students were expected to know more about their vocation in less time than other majors. Either I had picked the wrong career, or life was going to be completely inequitable from here on out.

I never hid the fact that I was clueless. I openly confessed my lack of medical knowledge, and suggested they visit the campus infirmary to get *real* medical care instead. Oddly enough, that never seemed to deter anyone. Once, when I refused to remove a splinter for Miss Zoo Beta Poo, she flounced away, muttering in disgust, "Geez! I thought you wanted to be a nurse!"

She was right. I *wanted* to be a nurse. If I already knew how to be one, I wouldn't have to be in school right now. No one seemed to see the logic in that but me. Sheesh. It was like the Red Cross fire safety plan all over again.

The truth was, I wasn't sure I could handle being a nurse. I had hardly handled a Band-Aid up to that point. The only medical experience I had to speak of was garnered during a high school sleepover when I pierced my BFF's ear. That's right. Ear, as in singular. (Read on.)

Most girls go to Claire's or a doctor's office to get their ears pierced. That would have been too boring. Instead, my BFF and I decided it would be way more fun to do it ourselves…on a whim… in the middle of the night. That's rarely a good combination.

Pretending to know what I was doing, I carefully eyeballed her earlobes and placed a mark in the center of each lobe with a Sharpie. Next, I froze her skin with an ice cube, the only numbing agent legally available to teenage anesthesiologists. When my friend was unable to feel my thumbnail pressing into her earlobe (the home piercing gold standard), I closed my eyes and plunged the thick metal corsage pin into the marked target with all the confidence of Dr. Oz cracking a chest (except I doubt he closes his eyes).

The procedure was going well right up until she heard the needle make a loud crunching noise as it passed through her skin. She almost threw up. Only one ear was done, but so was she. That was the beginning, as well as the end, of my surgical residency.

Over time, it became apparent that nursing required more than just a proclivity for math and science. There was an emotional component expected as well. What other major had that? I should have known. If I heard it once I heard it a thousand times: "You must have gone into nursing because you are a *people person.*" What did that even mean? Was every student who wanted to be a nurse a "people person"? And what is the plural form of that, I wonder. "People people?" Who knows.

Were accountants required to be dull? Were engineers required to be frugal? The inconsistencies were so maddening that if I heard the phrase "people person" one more time, I thought I was going to throw up.

Naively, I thought it would be enough to excel academically, but that wasn't enough at all. Nurses were expected to be "nurturers" - empathetic, kind-hearted creatures who "cared." I thought having compassion for all living creatures, great and small, was a vocation strictly reserved for veterinarians.

How was I going to be graded on that anyhow? Had anyone ever gotten an F in empathy? I was afraid to find out.

Either way, the whole concept was an outdated notion not backed by any scientific data that I was aware of, and should have been a requirement best left to the days of blue capes and white tights.

I may not have had compassion oozing from every pore, but I did have something else to offer patients that none of my classmates had. During one of my clinical rotations, I was called into my professor's office to discuss "an important matter." I panicked. What if I had killed someone? That was my biggest fear as a nursing student, something accounting majors never have to worry about. I stepped into my professor's office and the conversation went like this:

Professor: "Sally, when I interviewed the patients you took care of in your clinical rotation, they all had the same thing to say about you."

Me: Whew. They were talking. Dead people don't talk.

Professor: "They all said you made them laugh."
Me: They may not be dead but I will be. My father always told me to keep my silly side under wraps. He warned me that if I laughed too much others would see me as unintelligent. Great. There goes my scholarship and my independence.
Professor: "They also said that, after you made them laugh, they *felt better.*"
Me: Felt better? That's good, right? At least that's not dead. Whew. Don't scare me like that.

My professor confirmed that indeed, nurses *were* allowed to laugh and that didn't mean you were stupid. Up until that moment, my only experience with humor in a medical setting was obtained the summer before college, when I was a secretary in the surgery department. My duties required me to carry freshly amputated limbs to the pathology lab for review. I announced my presence in the lab by saying, "Hello there! I'm putting my best foot forward!" Sometimes I'd struggle with the door and say, "Hey, can I get a leg up," or "could you give me a hand?" All corny jokes to be sure, but it made the pathologists laugh. (If you know any pathologists personally, you'd know that's quite a feat. They're a tough crowd.)

It turned out that nursing was the perfect vocation for me after all. I could save lives and hone my goofy sense of humor all at the same time. What a relief.

At the end of my freshman year, I headed home, satisfied that I had chosen the right profession. When I didn't have a ride to the airport, someone suggested I ask a guy named Fred for a lift. Fred was a Junior I had met at the beginning of the school year at a campus fellowship mixer. He was a nice enough guy, but let's just say, Fred's most endearing quality was that he had a car.

Fred was a nerdy engineering physics major who claimed to study eighty hours a week. He was under-dressed and under-kempt, but didn't seem to know it. Fred possessed an underwhelming personality and an overzealous heart for Jesus, both evident at our first meeting. Fred talked loudly and laughed obnoxiously, slapping his knee while he guffawed, something I'd only seen on the show *Hee Haw*.*

Fred wore shiny polyester shirts with short gym shorts and yellow-striped tube socks. With his poor wardrobe and lack of social skills, I figured that he'd be free on Friday night to make the drive to the airport. I figured correctly.

Fred picked me up in his burnt orange Duster as promised. We chatted as he drove, mostly about his mind-bending mathematical algorithms and brainy class-mates, two of whom were building time machines. As if that weren't sufficiently dull, he droned on and on about his severe allergies to grass and all living plants.

Hee Haw is the syndicated television equivalent of a Jeff Foxworthy variety show on slapstick steroids. If you can picture Larry the Cable Guy telling Boozy Bumpkin jokes and crooning in the cornfields, you've just seen Hee Haw in your mind. No need to tune in. (FYI, it was my in-laws favorite show.)

With conversation this riveting, I figured he was probably allergic to human beings as well.

As though to demonstrate his allergic tendencies, he drummed up a sneeze of seismic proportions. I watched in absolute horror as he cranked down the window and hocked out a bucket-full of thick green mucous at sixty miles an hour. The hamster-sized blob immediately slapped back onto the window, drizzling a thick layer of disgusting phlegm across the windowpane for the remainder of the twenty-minute trip. I looked away the whole time, trying not to be sick. I got out of the car and thanked him for the ride, desperately wishing I had taken the bus.

Two years later, we were married.

Chapter 7

Kids R'~~nt~~ Us

"Everybody knows how to raise children, except
the people who have them."
P.J. O'Rourke

I know lots of people have children, but I wasn't sure I ever wanted to be one of those people. The whole big Greek family idea was appealing, right until I figured out that you have to have kids to accomplish that. I wasn't a big fan of kids, especially whiny ones (as you well know). Oh sure, there were a couple I liked, but as a whole, I thought they were highly overrated. In all fairness, however, it wasn't the child that I disliked; it was the stuff that kids did on a minute-by-minute basis that irked me to death. I would have loved children if they were not so, well, childish.

As a result, I came up with a brilliant idea for a specialty chain of restaurants. It would be called Kids R'nt Us, the antithesis of child-friendly Kids-R-Us because it would be very UN-friendly to kids. In theory, KRU would be to childless folks what Buffalo Wild Wings is to sports fans whose eyes are glued to zillions of pixels while scarfing down enough chicken grease to clog a kitchen sink.

This spark of genius was the result of numerous dining experiences completely ruined by other people's obnoxious children. No matter the restaurant, I was relentlessly persecuted by inconsolable rug rats and their parents' half-hearted and extremely ineffective "shushing." I wasn't planning on having to shush tiny people myself in the near future, if ever. Happily childfree and planning on remaining that way, I looked for places to eat that catered to like-minded individuals. If I ever *did* decide to procreate, my children would be perfectly behaved in public. *Naturally.*

There was no guilt on my part about feeling this way. As far as I could tell, nobody really liked infants in the first place. All one had to do was witness a woman with an armful of fussy baby scanning for her seat on an airplane to garner that assumption.

When faced with the potential of having an inconsolable screamer next to them for three hours, passengers hold their breath and look away. At this point, their thoughts are loud enough to hear, as they hope against hope that Baby Mama will boogie on down the aisle, letting someone else deal with the potentially communicable baby cooties.

As a frequent flier, I'd seen the reaction a hundred times. I tried to keep a running list of mental notes on appropriate behavior should I be the next one to lose at the Bambino Lottery. Here's what I learned: if you happen to be the unlucky loser in the sorry-but-you-are-sitting-next-to-the-baby game, it is socially polite to force a wry smile in front of the mother so you don't look like a total loser. At the same time, it is acceptable, if not expected, to privately grimace at the rest of the passengers to let them feel your pain as you take one for the flying team. It's complicated, but doable.

Restaurants were as unpleasant a place to have children in as airplanes were in my opinion. I simply didn't have the tolerance to sit next to a child who could, and would, generate more noise than an 80's rock concert during dinner. Oh sure, I could force a wry smile as I sat down, but the escalating racket, not to mention the booths filled with macaroni and cheese droppings, pushed me over the edge on more than one occasion. I could barely swallow because my mind was too focused on why people let their children behave so poorly in restaurants. "Who on earth thinks it's acceptable to let their kids be so loud in public?" I fumed. The general adult population had no choice but to tolerate child abuse, in the auditory sense, that is.

Noise was merely the tip of the irritation iceberg. I could not only see and hear the snot-nosed nuisances, I could feel them too. Smiley, hair-brained hostesses never failed to place me within arm's reach of the most hyperactive five year old alive. I wondered if there was a cosmic seating chart designed to aggravate me as much as possible by seating me next to small children who were either sick or haven't slept in two weeks. Or perhaps every hostess in the land could smell my fear and did it on purpose to drive me crazy. In either case, it worked.

As soon as I sat down, Adam ADD began jumping on the vinyl-covered booth, the kind where his seat was unavoidably attached to mine on the other side. It was like trying to eat with a miniature drum line marching up and down my spinal cord. I found myself chewing to the pulse of his expensive little Air Jordans, vowing to eat somewhere else next time around.

Mr. Hyperdrive was rarely an only child. He was typically accompanied by his equally annoying sister, Little Miss Nosey. Not to be outdone by her overly rambunctious brother, Sinister Sissy had plenty of her own ideas when it came to ruining my meal. When she wasn't chattering like a squirrel on amphetamines, she made it her business to peer over the seat, directly into the back of my head. I could feel her beady little eyes drilling holes into my skull, mining the last ounce of patience from my brain as I tried to enjoy my now-Unhappy-Meal. "Raised by wolves," I declared inwardly, wincing as each nugget was chewed with the etiquette of hogs at a trough.

As if to signal closure, there was the suck-the-cup-dry-through-the-straw-until-someone-tells-you-to-stop routine. It was all I could do to keep from hurling my arms back over my head, grabbing Suzy Slurper by her skinny little neck, and flipping her onto my table like a world federation wrestler. One swift takedown would shock the childishness right out of her. "Aha! I knew you were back there!" I would scowl between my clenched teeth, an inch from that snotty freckled nose. "I am paying good money for this food and you have ruined it for me! You owe me twenty bucks kiddo…cough it up!"

In the end, I decided that kids weren't really to blame. Poor parenting must be at the heart of the issue. Bratty begets bratty, just like whining begets whining. Obnoxious brats were inevitably raised by incompetent DNA-passers with a general lack of consideration for society.

Parents who were the slightest bit polite would banish their preschool pests to the car while everyone else finished eating in solace. On more than one occasion, my father threatened to send me to the car if I became a menace during our weekly post-church ritual of chicken fried steak at the local Bonanza. I'll admit, the car-banishing threat seemed a little harsh (it never actually happened because my mother routinely protested), but at least my father was concerned for the unsuspecting strangers around him. "Other people are just as important as you are," he sternly admonished on more than one occasion.

Well-behaved children were a rarity in every arena. One Sunday, I sat in church directly in front of a toddler who's incessant kicking made it practically impossible to sing on beat. Little Drummer Boy was, no doubt, related to Baby Babble-On, the verbose six-month-old who tainted the entire service with her incessant cooing.

Holy Cow! How in heaven's name was I supposed to worship with all that racket going on? If they weren't directly behind my line of sight, I would have shot them a dirty look or two. I may have sprained my neck to do so, but it would have been worth it to let them know what a pain in the neck they had been to me. Didn't they know they were disturbing my time with Almighty God? I decided to withhold the killer look, deciding it would be more satisfying to run into them in person, perhaps in the fellowship hall near the punch and cookies. That would have given me the opportunity to glare at them directly and cluck my tongue in disgust at their punch-stained shirts and crumbly chins.

Speaking of stains, I couldn't believe people let their children run around with soiled clothing and in public no less. Well-behaved children would reflect good parenting by being well-groomed at all times. No one likes a sloppy baby, least of all me. Hourly bib changes would be a good idea, something the government should mandate if parents weren't willing to do it themselves. If there wasn't a Parental Manual For The Planet there should be one, and bib changes would be Article One, Section One. That clause would be directly followed by Article Two, which would expressly prohibit preschoolers from blowing snot bubbles in the presence of others, especially at the dinner table.

I didn't think I was asking for too much. I wasn't asking for special rights, just equal rights for singles, YUPpies (Young Urban Professionals), and the DINKs (Dual Income No Kids) of this world who are trying to gulp down a bite or two in relative (or non-relative, as the case may be) peace. That's when my brilliant idea hit me: I'll make a place where it is truly IMPOSSIBLE to be annoyed by children during a meal. That's how and Kids R'nt Us was born.

The details quickly fell into place. The front door would include a sign that says "You must be this tall to eat at this establishment," and make it 5'0" or more. (Short people would be judged on a case-by-case basis.) Perhaps I would hire a welcome greeter, similar to Wal-Mart (but one who can still see and hear), functioning for all practical purposes as a Baby Bouncer. This was necessary in case the occasional obtuse, chronically-sleep-deprived parent tried to sneak a diaper-donned nuisance in for a snack. When denied admittance, they would look quizzically through the front door wondering why their little "angel" was being denied entrance into my private gastronomical club. "What?" they would protest, "Little Bratty Boo Boo not allowed?? How can this be?" There would be sobbing and gnashing of teeth (or gums, depending on their current dentition). My Baby Bouncer would be specially trained in how to turn away such delinquents, launching into a full-scale tutorial as to why children were ruining the dining experience of adults on planet Earth. I would do the talking myself, but that would take entirely too much of my time. After all, I had a restaurant to run.

Even couples with children would be clamoring for a reservation in my unique eatery precisely because their children *were not* allowed. With tears of joy, they would leave Thing 1 and Thing 2 behind so they could eat at a safe distance from their own cranky food-flingers, as well as societal menaces produced by other un-self-aware breeders. In my establishment, a quiet, romantic dinner was a sure thing. No more pleading for a table two zip codes away from babies whose decibels had reached OSHA hazard levels. Diners would marvel at the clean tables, free from cheap waxy crayons, colored crazy straws and broken graham crackers. They could actually hear the delightful music being piped in, rather than the incessant wailing and whining of overly-tired munchkins who missed their midday nap.

No one would ever hear another aggravating chorus of "Can I have a gum ball?" as patrons exited. In my restaurant, there would be no lobby gumball machine with brightly colored roller coaster tracks and fancy-schmancy lights designed to nickel and dime parents out of their last ounce of dignity. Gumballs are a dessert for the entitled. Only spoiled, ungrateful kids would ask for jaw-breaking candy designed to induce a costly and time-consuming visit to the dentist. My restaurant would not be party to such selfish behavior. Yes, even post-breeders would look upon Kids R'nt Us as a much-needed refuge.

They wouldn't be alone. College students could plug into their alternative universe, unconcerned about stepping on stray noodles or sticky gummy bears which might turn their expensive boots into an Ugg-ly mess. The AARP crowd would frequent KRU as well, provided, of course, we opened early enough for them to catch Wheel of Fortune and clap their lights out by 8:00 p.m. Going global wasn't entirely out of the question. No one liked to eat near a whiny little kid, regardless of what language they whined in.

I may not have been a business major, but I was on to something big. That is, right until I was informed that this is the basic function of a bar.

Oh well. So much for great ideas.

Chapter 8

Every Girl's ~~Wake Up You're Having a Bad~~ Dream Wedding

"I love being married. It's so great to find that one special person you want to annoy for the rest of your life."
Rita Rudner

Fred popped the question after dating for one year. Two minutes later, I had twenty Bridal magazines spread across my bed. You know the kind, where everyone looks so sculpted and manicured it makes you wanna throw up (and then elope). Every glossy page is filled with blindingly white smiles and a thick coat of happily-ever-after spray tan. Those magazines ought to come with a front-page disclaimer from the Marital General:

DO NOT TRY THIS AT HOME. THE PEOPLE ON THESE PAGES ARE NOT REAL. THEY ARE PAID MODELS. HALF OF ALL MARRIAGES END IN DIVORCE. PURCHASING THE PRODUCTS

CONTAINED HEREIN WILL NOT GUARANTEE THE HAPPILY-EVER-AFTER YOU SO DESPERATELY WANT AND HAVE BEEN DUPED INTO BELIEVING IS POSSIBLE FROM WATCHING TOO MANY SHOWS ON THE W-NETWORK.

Even if a warning were printed on the cover in gigantic red letters, it wouldn't matter. No one would pay attention, just like the pointless warnings on cigarette packs. Has anyone ever NOT bought cigarettes because of the tiny little warning label on the package? If someone is close enough to read the fine print, it means they've already bought the goods and are not about to heed some lame after-the-fact warning printed on the package.

Weddings used to be much simpler affairs than they are today, at least in my social sphere. I didn't know anyone personally who was wealthy enough to tie the knot in an extravagant Italian Villa, with synchronized swans and dazzling red fireworks in the shape of a heart like you see on TV. These days, the whole bridal party looks camera-ready, as though they just stepped out of a Ralph Lauren catalog. One has to wonder if today's elegant brides choose their bridesmaids out of true friendship or because they have the potential to be a stunning addition to their coffee table wedding album.

In search of our own happily-ever-after, Fred and I were married during a late December sunset, in the small plain church I grew up in. The building wasn't much to look at, a sort of Frank-Lloyd-Wright-meets-Amish structure with a few squares of colored glass to make it churchy looking. Thankfully, the glow of evening shone through windows framed by strands of white holiday lights which covered a multitude of architectural sins. The pretty Christmas decorations were still up, which gave the sanctuary what a bra gives to Dolly Parton; a much needed lift.

Perhaps it would have been different had I hired a wedding planner, as is the custom today. I planned my own wedding, down to the last detail. It never even occurred to me to have my big day orchestrated by some flamboyant, larger-than-life wedding planner who talked with their hands more than their mouth. Compared to anything you can see on cable TV these days, our wedding was downright boring.

Our ceremony was beautiful, and it took place on the last day of the calendar year, which meant my father gave away a daughter and a whole year of tax deductions on the same day. There was much speculation as to which was more painful.

Many little girls plan their wedding day years ahead of time. Not me. Playing bride was in the same category as playing with dolls that cried and whined. Of course, I wanted to look like a princess on my big day like every other girl (especially after I saw Princess Diana's hullabaloo), but it never crossed my mind to make a part-time career out of hunting down the perfect wedding dress. I had no desire to spend hours upon hours fretting over frocks that cost as much as a new car. Why say "yes to that stress?"

I find it a little ridiculous that today's brides drag an entourage the size of Vermont to the bridal salon, supposedly for moral support (or financial aide, it's not always clear which). They sip champagne and try on gowns that look like something out of a Broadway production of *The Little Mermaid*. These brides have fantastical visions of themselves as international runway models sashaying down the aisle to their groom. Nothing short of spectacular will do.

When I got married, we wore one wedding dress. Just one. No one changed into twelve different gowns with a price tag rivaling the national debt. Back then, wedding dresses were not quite as fancy either, and most of them still had sleeves,* a fashion trend that has gone the way of girdles and good manners. Even though strapless dresses were the up and coming rage, I would never have considered wearing one. My father once said, "Nice girls don't bare that much skin on their wedding day," so I covered my arms with the modesty of a nun at a brothel.

Dresses are not the only way in which brides have upped the glamour. Fashion-savvy brides have a

---

* Who has taken it upon themselves to cut off all the sleeves on wedding gowns? Note to designers: bring the sleeves back. Not all brides were meant to go strapless.

professional stylist work their hair into a fabulous coif for their big day. Not me. It was too much of a risk.

The day of my senior prom, I had my hair professionally styled which turned out to be a disastrous waste of time and money.

Two hours before my date was to pick me up, I sat in a pumped-up pink pleather chair with my back to the mirror, for what felt like an eternity. Oddly enough, all the hairdressers had plant names, so Rose washed, Fern teased, and Iris pinned my Rapunzel-length locks into a masterful creation. At least that's what I *thought* was happening.

When my chair was finally swiveled around for the "big reveal," I was horrified at my own reflection. I didn't recognize the girl in the mirror. What was *supposed* to be a "simple up-do" had turned into the blond Leaning Tower of Pisa, tall enough to conceal a giant poodle.

Too numb to balk (or in a state of catatonic shock, I can't remember which), I sat in polite silence while the beauty operator sprayed my head with enough shellac to withstand the gale forces of a clipper ship. The hairspray was still sticky as I raced toward my car, ripping out every bobby pin as fast as I could, praying there was enough time to start over before my date arrived.

So, on my wedding day, I decided it was much safer to wash my own hair and set it with the hot rollers my mother had purchased for me in the seventh grade. Before crowning my home-done hairdo with a white tulle veil, I added a small squirt of hair spray that touted a "comb-able hold."*

In fact, I took a decidedly more DIY approach to the whole thing, not just my hair. As far as make-up, I barely wore any. I didn't even own foundation or cover-up, since my ten minute routine didn't allow for the time consuming process of facial fancying. (More confusion from the world of make-up. I thought a foundation is what you build a house on, and cover-up was a beach garment. Argh.) Blush was not in my make-up arsenal either, since my cheeks had a "naturally rosy" glow. (That's a nice way of saying red and blotchy.) This inherited trait is pretty when you're young, but loses its appeal when you look like Mrs. Claus, and even NASA-strength laser treatments aren't strong enough to eradicate it.

In keeping with the au naturel, come-as-you-are look, I skipped the tanning booth, bikini wax, and pedicure. However, at my mother's suggestion, I splurged on a professional manicure the morning of the wedding. It seemed like a brilliant idea. However, once again, the salon yielded catastrophic results. Daisy, the manicurist, insisted on painting my nails "bridal white," a pearlescent polish I'd only seen on excessively tanned old ladies in Florida. I vowed to take it off the moment I said, "I do."

So my only adornment for the wedding was a quick coat of black mascara, plain blue eye shadow, and shiny clear lip-gloss from Mary Kay, which I loved

---

* What in the world is a comb-able hold? I thought the whole point was to freeze your hair so you could NOT drag a comb through it if you tried. Would somebody please explain this to me?

but rarely wore since my mother insisted it smelled like a public restroom. In essence, I've taken more time getting ready for trick-or-treating than I did to tie the knot.

Fred let me do all the planning for the wedding. He didn't have much of an opinion in the way of invitations, flowers, or music because he didn't even know we *needed* invitations, flowers, or music. I'm not sure he'd ever been to a wedding before.

I relied heavily on my mother for those details. My mother has fabulous taste and gave great advice about the ceremony, though she rarely offered advice on matrimony itself. She did, however, profess three highly valuable tips in regards to marriage:

1) Never register for anything that can't go in the dishwasher. (Check)

2) Refrain from cooking your new husband breakfast every morning in the early years of marriage. He will expect it forever, and it is virtually impossible to do once the children arrive. (Check)

3) It's just as easy to marry a rich man as it is to marry a poor one. (Oh well, two out of three ain't bad.)

For the most part, Fred's eyes glazed over like blue Krispy Kremes when discussing the wedding, until I mentioned there would be food at the reception. Suddenly the whole event became much more palatable.

Just when I was about to ask him to weigh in on the menu, I recalled how an older lady asked him what his favorite dish was so his new bride could learn how to make it (like in the old days, when people actually cooked). With gusto, Fred replied, "Ma'am, I just love beanie weenies!" slapping his knee with a snort and a smile. He was as serious as a heart attack. So I kept my mouth shut about the wedding menu, except to whisper a prayer of thanks that my fiancé's culinary bar was set so low I could practically walk over it.

My mother wanted a formal receiving line. Fred hated the idea of a formal receiving line. In fact, he hated the idea of a formal *anything*. Naturally, my mother won out. After all, the glorious occasion of a wedding *is* a milestone for parents to enjoy as well as the bride and groom. A wedding is a celebration to relish and savor for sentimental reasons. It is also imperative that whoever paid for it milk every cent out of the dollar-per-minute expense laid out for the day.

A small orchestra played during the traditional sit-down dinner reception, a drawn out affair which lasted far too long in Fred's estimation. Champagne toasts and speeches from the bridal party got on his last nerve.

By the time the dancing began, I could tell Fred had run out of patience. The band would have played all night if it weren't for my eager husband's insistent slashing motion across his throat with his finger, emphatically signaling the band to "wrap it up" and go home. I watched with amusement as my mom and Fred played emotional Ping-Pong with the band director for hours. My mother politely asked for "one more song" while Fred's exaggerated gestures told the instrumentalists in no uncertain terms that the highly anticipated wedding night needed to start sooner rather than later.

All in all, our wedding was a beautiful occasion. There was no bridal meltdown, no wedding party drama, and no wedding crashers (that we were aware of). Our cake was not in the shape of the Hancock building, and there was no planned lunar eclipse in celebration of our nuptials, but we said our vows and we meant them. Odd as it may sound, we were actually interested in getting married rather than having a wedding. It would have made for horrible reality television.

That's not to say I wouldn't change several very important things if I had the chance to do it all over again.

First, I would hire a *quality* videographer to capture the day on film. When people watch your wedding video, they shouldn't feel queasy and be prompted to ask if you got married on a roller coaster. An armadillo with a camera strapped to its back would have produced steadier footage than our videographer. What a waste of a good fifty bucks.

Secondly, I would have spent more than fifteen minutes getting ready for the most important day of my life. Apparently, it didn't occur to me that everyone

I knew, not to mention a professional photographer, would be there, snapping photos for eternal posterity.

My less-than-glam look could have been partially attributed to twenty-some years of an out-the-door beauty routine, but I knew it went deeper than that. I simply didn't feel like getting glammed up in the first place.

Two weeks before the wedding, I took my father with me for my final fitting. I was really looking forward to this moment because I had grand visions of my would-be Pa gasping, perhaps even tearing up, at the sight of his little girl all grown up as a beautiful bride-to-be.

When I came out of the dressing room he looked at me for a moment, and then asked my mother, *out loud*, "What size is that dress?" All I heard after that was an incredulous groan, a hopeless sigh, and a disappointed throat clearing. If he said anything after that I didn't notice.

My mother and the entourage of shop ladies stepped up with all the right accolades and words of affirmation, but it fell on deaf ears. Those few stinging words let all the emotional air out of my princess balloon, and I never looked at the dress the same way again.

Why is it that we always hear the negative comments, even if they are hidden among a thousand good ones? Julia Roberts' character in *Pretty Woman* said, "It's easier to believe the bad stuff." That is so true, especially when it comes from people we care about.

Thankfully, Fred thought I was (and still am) a stunning bride. That's all that should have mattered in the first place. I have since forbidden him to have corrective eye surgery. Ever.

Oh, and finally, the last thing I would change... if my brand new mother-in-law asked, during the after-ceremony photo op, that I, the bride, "step out of the picture so I can get a photo of our family, just *our* family, dear," I would have politely, but firmly, told her "no." And perhaps a few other things.

Chapter 9

I Married Fred ~~Flintstone~~

*"Marriage is like a 5000 piece jigsaw puzzle.
All sky."*
Cathy Ladman

Fred may have lacked a bit of finesse when we got married, but that didn't matter to me one bit. After all, most men require a bit of "tweaking" here and there along the way, especially when they are forced to share their man cave with a female.

It wasn't like we were combining households, because neither of us had anything to bring to the marriage but our respective stereos. There was no fighting over who kept what ugly furniture or whose dishes to keep because we were too young to have accumulated any of that yet. I practically had to pull a pacifier out of my mouth to say my vows.

It was more of a lifestyle thing, like realizing that

wearing tube socks and shorts to a wedding might not be appropriate, especially now that you had a wife on your arm. It took great amounts of convincing to get Fred to buy a nice pair of shoes in addition to his Payless pair ("But Sal, you can only wear one pair at a time!"). He gave in eventually, even splurging on a really *nice* pair of tube socks to go with his new shoes. It was a baby step, but it was progress none the less.

Anything (or any*one*, I should say) can benefit from a fresh coat of paint, and that's all Fred really needed. I've always liked to paint, so taking on a hub-ject (a husband-project) was right up my alley. Fred seemed a little mystified by all the fuss, but I'm not sure *any* man (or woman for that matter) knows what he's getting into when the "I do's" are said. Adam wasn't even *awake* when he got a wife, so the fact that Fred was conscious when we got married put him way ahead of the curve.

I embraced my new husband's rough edges, like Wilma embraced Fred's. She and I understood our Freds. They both had a sweet and salty mix of idio-syncrasies which made them endearing, and challenging, all at the same time.

For example, when both Freds walked through the door from work, they affectionately bellowed our names loudly (Wilma...Sally!!!) as though we were in Canada. Endearing, in that they can't wait to see us. Challenging, to say the least, because our first apartment was so small we could see each other from every square inch. A whisper would have been enough to get my attention. (And the neighbor's.)

"What's for dinner?" was the overly-enthusiastic greeting both our Fred's bellowed upon return from work. Watching the clock, I braced myself for the inevitable vocal blast, securing nearby breakables, lest they resonate off the shelf with his signature surround sound. He has since toned it down a bit. Either that or my hearing aids aren't working properly.

However, it was almost impossible to get mad at my sweet hungry subwoofer. Although the food was never fancy, he was always eager to ingest it with delight as though it were.

We couldn't afford Brontosaurus burgers those first few years, but it never mattered to Fred. He was grateful for anything. I didn't have to produce gourmet fare to make him happy. He valued quantity over quality, timing over taste. The food didn't even have to be hot. It just had to be ready the minute he walked through the door. It didn't take long to learn that Fred's idea of fast food was to open the refrigerator door and begin chewing. Even Wilma could appreciate that.

Fred Flintstone worked in a quarry, and was presumably a rock scientist. My Fred was a true rock-et scientist, a brilliant engineer who is as savvy with numbers as I am at a shoe sale. Fred solves problems for a living; problems most mortals would classify as hieroglyphics from a galaxy far, far away.

As amazing as his problem-solving skills were, they came to a screeching halt the moment he entered a closet. In other words, Fred's ability to assemble a color-coordinated wardrobe was, shall we say, lacking. (That's way too nice. I'm just gonna say it. He was clueless.) Poor Fred had no fashion sense at all. I mean zero. If you doubt the stereotype, read a Dilbert comic strip. The opinion is universal.

I had sincerely hoped Fred's penchant for yellow-striped tube socks and polyester shirts were merely a youthful phase of indiscriminate dressing, a fad that would disappear with his bachelorhood. Sadly, it was not. This became painfully obvious when he repeatedly held up shirts and pants as he got dressed in the morning asking, "Do these greens match?"*

In an effort to help my cute but clueless groom dress himself, I thought about designing a clothing line for fashion-deficient men like Fred. I would call it Garengineers. The concept is similar to Garanimals, a line of clothing where children match giraffes to kangaroos or lions to zebras, in order to coordinate an outfit. With brainy precision, engineers could match pocket protectors and slide rules, or calculators and mechanical pencils, nerdy stuff they'd recognize.

If it was a success, I could expand, offering hope to other wardrobe-challenged professionals like accountants and actuaries. It was a great idea, but alas,

* *I should have known color wasn't his thing. During our first date, he dreamily declared "you have the most beautiful blue eyes I've ever seen." My eyes are green.*

that entrepreneurial venture would have to wait until after I opened my Kids R'nt Us restaurant chain. So many ideas, so little time.

Thankfully, Fred has gotten way better over the years. I even let him buy his own clothes now. Not all engineers have grown in that way. He gets lots of accolades for his smarts these days, so I have to sit through engineering award dinners, which I call MDB's for Men Dressing Badly. He laughs along with me. Poor dear has lost his long term memory.

There is no doubt that Fred thinks like a genius, except for the time he could not figure out why his computer printer would not print out his Master's thesis. He called ten different people asking for advice. Turns out he had forgotten to plug the printer into the wall.   Once I, er, Fred figured that out, he plugged the cord into the socket and the printer began to spew out equations that only Einstein could understand. Go figure. I'm just thankful the problem was solved before he dialed up my father, who was next in line on the help list. I would have never heard the end of it.

It was then that I realized for some people, common sense isn't all that common. Fred is one of those people. This fact was confirmed when he changed the oil in our car for the first time. Frugal Fred insisted on doing it himself, in hopes of keeping to our extremely tight budget. I wasn't sure it was such a good idea after the printer incident, but he insisted. Fred had grown up with very little material wealth and was accustomed to living on the cheap. I admired his cost-cutting efforts (after all, I had shoes to buy), but when he drained the dirty oil and forgot to put a drip pan underneath, I was a little less enthusiastic. It was even harder to cheer him on after he poured in several quarts of new oil, forgetting to replace the plug underneath before doing so. I think BP spent less time cleaning up the Gulf than we did cleaning up our driveway. One thing I always knew for sure. Fred's heart was in the right place even if the oil plug wasn't.

Like most married couples, Fred and I differ in the way we think, but not just due to gender differences. Our different skill sets affected how we think as well. As an engineer, Fred thinks in terms of invisible molecules (protons, neutrons) and their affect on gravitational pull. As a nurse, I think in terms of visible molecules (skin, muscles, fat cells) and the affect gravity has on them. When he talks about lift and drag, his mind automatically turns to aviation. Mine automatically turns to Spanx.

Despite our differences, Fred and I both went to the alter hoping for a peaceful, carefree marriage with like-minded communication and happiness. (Who doesn't?) That's why it was surprising that our first year of wed*lock* had so many ups and downs. The words wed and lock together should have been a clue that the word *escape* was going to cross our minds at some point.

I had an overly romanticized vision of what marriage would be like, and Fred didn't really know what to envision at all. On top of that, Fred and I both lacked the consistent ability to communicate like mature adults. (This was especially evident when the other person was acting like such a childish jerk.)

In fact, part of me believes that the crushing disappointment of less-than-fairytale marital bliss would have separated our lives forever had it not been for our common faith and the extensive premarital counseling Fred insisted upon. Premarital counseling is to marriage what the Red Cross babysitting course is to childcare. It's no guarantee of success, but somehow you feel the odds are stacked in your favor if you've been through it. (There's no laminated card, however, which would have been a nice touch.)

Our counselors gave us reading assignments and a battery of personality tests to see how compatible we are. (He's an in-y, I'm an out-y.) No topic was off limits. We discussed everything from finances to foods, and family traditions to favorite colors. Mine happens to be white, which Fred vehemently insisted is not a color, but the total absence of color. (A foreshadow of the caliber of arguments to come.)

We covered conflict resolution, but I must have been listening as closely to this information as I was to the bath-giving portion of the Red Cross course. Fred and I were given typical conflict scenarios and encouraged to role-play possible resolutions as husband and wife.   It felt a bit like playing Virtual Matrimony, a video game for fiancés, except that you can't blow up your partner or hit END GAME when they make a move you don't like. (Shoot.)

One particularly interesting discussion entailed the division of household chores. We both came from traditional homes where the fathers earned the paycheck, and the mothers did the cruddy jobs or "women's work" as my father called it.   Fred and I touted ourselves as a modern, progressive couple out to change history.   After all, I had an education and planned to use it.   With puffed-up pride, we declared ourselves "above that mentality," and promised to assign roles based on capability and interest rather than standard male/female roles.   Unfortunately, that progress came to a screeching halt when I was assigned all the cooking, cleaning, and laundry. (That's another book entirely.)

In an effort to foster communication, our counselors challenged us to forgo television for our entire first year of marriage. (Besides, who had time for TV now that I had so many loads of laundry to do?)   Rather than night after night of parallel viewing, they suggested we engage in more emotionally connected alternatives, such as playing board games, reading to each other, and of course, lots and lots of sex.   Fred jumped all over that idea.   No wonder Fred was so gung-ho about the premarital program.

Surprisingly,   we   enjoyed   the   challenge, although several friends told us we were practically un-American   for   not   having   a   TV.   Fred   and   I laughed when the local newspaper ran a cover story about a couple in Florida who were living without a television - on purpose - as though they had just slithered out of Area 51. We could have been famous and we didn't even know it.

During one of our sessions, I discovered that Fred was an Eagle Scout. It turns out he had not only been an Eagle Scout, but part of a select group of accomplished scouts who are bestowed an Indian name during a special ceremony. His Indian name was Apuit-cawilla-wilen-damogen, an impressive sounding title no doubt. It wasn't until *after* we were married that I learned it translated into "he who is easily confused." Oh.

One topic I wish had been included on the agenda was bathroom etiquette. I had no idea how much time men like to spend in the bathroom. I was mystified. You would think we didn't have chairs in the rest of the house. I finally rationalized this rather odd behavior by conceding that men are created in God's image, so it's only natural they would want to spend eternity on the throne.

By the end of our counseling, we had come to a unanimous decision on every forseeable marital topic with the gravity of a Supreme Court ruling. Every topic that is, except for having children. We broached the subject briefly, but did not delve into the matter as deeply as we should have. I brushed it off, hoping we could switch to more comfortable topics like how to spend money, assuming we would have some eventually.

For reasons I couldn't articulate to myself or anyone else, I wasn't completely sold on the idea of having children (if in doubt, review Chapter 7). It wasn't Fred I was concerned about, at least emotionally. From a physical standpoint, I was pretty certain that the brunt of childcare would fall on me. I wondered if naming a son Atom would help Fred know what to do with it so he could lend a hand in that department. (Might be worth a try someday.)

Rather, it was me I was concerned about. I wasn't entirely sure I could be a good mom. In fact, I was pretty sure I wasn't going to be. If playing with dolls was any indication of what kind of mother I would be, my only hope was having a kid with a full head of non-retractable hair that didn't need diapers or baths. Even then, I wasn't sure I could handle it.

Fred didn't express an overwhelming opinion on the matter either way, except to say that we should leave it open for future debate.

So, after a brief discussion, Fred and I reached the same nebulous verdict. We were both in violent agreement that while possible, but not altogether plausible, children may or may not be part of our matrimonial union.

Whew. Glad we clarified that.

Chapter 10

Housework is a ~~Royal~~ Pain

"Housework won't kill you, but why take a chance."
Phyllis Diller

Fred and I became homeowners during our third year of marital bliss. This was a rather stupid move considering we had very little money and the only house we could afford was something out of a home improvement reality show. I don't know why we were in such a hurry to buy a house. It's like rushing to the dentist office for a root canal that could be put off indefinitely.

The whole thing was my idea. Fred would have been happy living in a tent with a swinging lamp; I wanted a real house, a real kitchen, and real weeds to pull. Fred wanted me to be really happy, so we entered housebroke heaven with mutual naiveté.   We were nothing if not consistent.

We quickly realized that buying a house required a lot more than a down payment.   Before being handed the key, our realtor pulled out a ledger the length of his arm, instructing us to write sizable checks to people we'd never heard of for services we couldn't even recognize.   I actually paid someone to say the property was still *there*, an odd request considering I drove past it on my way to deliver the check.   (I want that gig.)

Such exercises in futility incensed me, like doing proofs in geometry class where you have to prove a circle is a circle when it's obvious to any idiot over three years of age that it's a stinkin' circle.   But, like a good student, I did what I was told even when I didn't understand why.   I always felt sorry for my geometry teacher.   Poor thing.   If she couldn't recognize a circle just by looking at it, she had bigger problems than I could solve.

As frustrating as that was, buying a home is the easy part.   Maintaining it is much more frustrating (and expensive), a fact I wish I'd known sooner rather than later.   Owning a house isn't the same as playing house, but I didn't know any better.   Perhaps I would have steered clear of homeownership forever if I'd known what was coming.

Looking back, I simply wasn't listening closely enough.   If I had been on my game, I would have noticed that the word **work** is almost always preceded by the words house and yard.

Clearly, I wasn't paying attention when my friends said things like "Bowling? I'd love to, but I have to go home and spend the entire weekend sweating over strenuous yard **work**. I have to do it now so that I can be rested in time to start all over again next weekend."

Apparently my ears were plugged when I asked friends to enjoy a night out and they replied, "A movie? Sounds like a blast, but I'm way behind on my house**work**. Maybe next year."

Let's face it, most long-term commitments are better disguised than homeownership. For example, no one would accept a marriage proposal if they heard "Will you marry me and share a lifetime of love**work**?" even if asked on bended knee.

In the same way, no couple in their right mind would have a baby if the obstetrician held up a squealing newborn and said, "Congratulations, you've just given birth to a beautiful bundle of baby**work!**" Such statements would lead to the end of family life as we know it.

On the other hand, when it comes to owning property, no one thinks twice about calling a spade a spade. Housework. Yard work. No cover-up. No conspiracy. How could I not have noticed? Perhaps it was because I never saw Barbie doing housework in her Malibu mansion. Come to think of it, I never saw Ken doing yard work either. I bet cousin Skipper did it all. That would explain why they kept her around.

It wasn't long before I realized Fred and I should have bought a small hotel instead of a house and lived in a couple of adjoining rooms. That way, I could have yard maintenance and maid service, but still say we owned our own place.

As much as I resented it, society expects a certain level of housekeeping in order to be considered a "responsible homeowner." That didn't necessarily mean the place had to be immaculate, but it did mean there was a general expectation of home hygiene. You didn't have to like it, but if you wanted to keep your friends, you had to do it. I came to the inevitable conclusion that most guests are leery of stopping by when your home isn't up to the basic health code. While free mushrooms may sound thrifty, serving them to guests is generally frowned upon when they're grown in the shower of the master bathroom.

To my surprise, I've discovered that some women don't mind housework. Some even find it enjoyable. I'm not one of those. Don't get me wrong; I love a clean house. I just don't like doing what's necessary to get it that way. I can think of a thousand things (two thousand, if pressed) that I'd rather be doing than sweeping and dusting.

I'm also not one of those women who insist the cleaning be done a certain way. I've actually known women to fire their housekeeper because they didn't clean the mirrors well enough. This begs the question; how clean can a mirror get? Or more to the point, how dirty can a mirror be in the first place? What are they doing to their mirror that I'm not doing to mine – sketching the Mona Lisa on it with a Sharpie? Trust me, if I had the luxury of a housekeeper, I would never complain about something as insignificant as a little mirror smudge here and there. In fact, staring into to a crystal clear reflection first thing in the morning can be a little depressing (unless my hair looks fabulous, a rarity, especially in the morning). So, a lackluster cleaning job would actually be doing me a favor. In poor lighting, a semi-clean mirror might cause my blurry morning vision to mistake my reflection for Heidi Klum on a bad day. Now that is a service I'm willing to pay for.

My mother is one of those women who loves to clean, or so it would appear. She was always a meticulous housekeeper, a total white-glover. Our house was never anything but immaculate. No dirt, no clutter, no dust bunnies.

I can remember honing my dusting skills by hanging out with my mom. Even now, the smell of furniture polish brings back strong childhood memories of putting my index finger in a dust cloth and wiping over nooks and crannies I didn't even know existed. My mother dusted so much I could have sworn she wore eau de Pledge (pronounced Pleje...with a French accent) instead of her signature Chanel No. 5.

Keeping our house visitor-ready was an all-consuming job. Perhaps my mom is one of many who has been falsely led to believe that "cleanliness is next to godliness."* If such a claim were true, then my mother was headed straight for the right hand of the Throne.

Not only could my mother clean like a champ, she could iron like nobody's business. She even ironed my father's handkerchiefs, a habit as outdated and disgusting as cloth handkerchiefs themselves. Sometimes the handkerchief didn't come out of the wash completely clean. I watched in horror as she inadvertently ironed the dried green globs right onto the cloth. Handkerchiefs have outlived their usefulness, just like cloth diapers. (The much-more-sanitary Kleenex train is here. Jump on it.)

Once a month, like clockwork (ahem, hor-

---

*This often-quoted pseudo-verse can be found in the lengthy book of fictional adages entitled Ramifications. Folks often look for that mythical verse in the adjacent book of Justifications, where they think they'll find the nonexistent verse that says "God only helps those who help themselves." (Just a little theological edumacation, if you will.)

mones...), my mom got a huge surge of energy and used it (and me) to rearrange the furniture. I mean totally rearrange. Not just switching a chair or two, but changing the entire floor plan. My father was always on a trip when she got like this, so I got to help lift the china cabinet and the piano, something every daughter looks forward to, especially late at night when the urge inevitably hit. My mother always took advantage of this opportunity to vacuum under the sofa and wipe down all the walls, something I only do when I move. I desperately wished she would just get cramps and lie down like the rest of us.

My mother used to say I would enjoy housework when I had my own home. She couldn't be more wrong. When I got my own house, I hated cleaning even more. The whole process is crazy-making because of its repetitive, cyclical nature. It's the same reason I could never be a hairdresser. The hair grows out, you cut it. The hair grows out, you cut it. The cycle never ends. It's never finished. In the same way, it's hard to for me to get excited about making a bed worthy of bouncing a quarter off of when I'm just going to mess it up a few hours later, especially if no one sees it in between.

My mother had a thousand throw pillows on every bed in the house, so I felt compelled to have them too. Throw pillows are a housekeeping nightmare, yet they are sold every day in this country proving there is still a demand. What a waste of time. On the bed, off the bed. On the bed, off the bed. You have to allow an extra three hours a day (1.5 for getting in bed at night, 1.5 for making it up in the morning) just for throw pillow relocation. That puts us east coasters to bed even later, thanks to the stupid time zone laws. I figured out that over my lifetime I have wasted over a thousand hours moving throw pillows. I could have spent that time doing the back of my hair.

So, given the expectations of *Better Homes and Gardens*, and my aversion to cleaning, I had a choice to make when it came to housework. Expert Dr. Phil* predicts that people typically do one of two things:

- they do exactly what their parents did

or

- they do the complete opposite

Translated, this meant that either I was going to be just like my mom and go all Martha Stewart (which is similar to "going postal" but with a dust mop instead of a semi-automatic weapon) or I would rebel against her white glove tendencies and end up in jail for breaking every environmental law on the books.

Contrary to Dr. Phil's predictions, I chose neither path. Instead, I came up with a compromise that embraced my own quirky imagination, as well as

---

* I'm suspicious that Dr. Phil and "they" are related.

my love of a clean house. I found an acceptable level of cleanliness which was somewhere between pristine and obscene by creating an alternate universe where cleaning house was less of a complete drudgery and more of a tolerable fantasy.

How? Well, I had seen old movies where royalty went out amongst the "common folk" incognito. They did it to know what it felt like to be, well, common. Resenting the spoils of privilege, they wanted to be seen for who they were instead of the crown they wore. Princess Diana was often quoted as saying she wanted to know how the "average person" lived, as evidenced by turning up in the palace kitchen to make her own sandwich from time to time. (I've never given it much thought, but come to think of it, I do feel quite average when making a sandwich.)

So, in honor of Her Royal Highness, I bobby-pinned a cheap rhinestone tiara* to my head (a treasured birthday gift from a friend who understood my neuroses), and began to clean house. An inexpensive can of glittery spray paint quickly transformed my toilet brush into a golden royal scepter, which I waved in Queenly

---

*I have since acquired much more elaborate tiaras via the Internet. Begrudgingly, Fred reminds me that traditionally, women do something spectacular to earn a tiara, like winning a beauty pageant or something archaic like that. I don't see the point. Why go to all the trouble of prancing about in an embarrassing swimsuit and answering silly questions about world peace when a credit card is all you need to acquire a sparkly crown on the World Wide Web. (Once again, thank you Mr. Gore.)

fashion as I dusted from room to room.

My regal ensemble was completed when I donned a pair of long white opera gloves, which not only added to the total monarchial look, but protected my skin from the prickly scrub brush which I carried scepter-style between bathrooms.

Adding a pair of sparkly earrings and a strand of pearls for effect, I threw on my best fuzzy house robe while I rubbed and scrubbed the entire house. So now, instead of being a bored housewife cleaning against her will, I was a princess who was pretending to be a commoner, to see what it was really like to be out of her gilded cage and clean the toilet of a princess.

My dizzying little psychosis made housework tolerable, if not entertaining. That is, right up until the postman rang the doorbell to deliver a package, and I answered it in my royal splendor. He has never looked at me the same way since.

Like I said, we should have bought a small hotel.

Chapter 11

To Breed or Not to Breed, That is the ~~Most Annoying~~ Question

"Parents are the last people on earth who ought to have children."
Samuel Butler

Purchasing a home caused "THE FAMILY ALERT SYSTEM" to go from yellow to red in a hurry. At least in *other* people's minds. We wondered if our industrial-sized washer and dryer gave visitors the impression that we were gearing up for a diaper-laundering frenzy. We were not. The jumbo-sized machines just happened to come with the house, which was previously owned by a petite elderly woman who could fit a year's worth of unmentionables in one load.

Soon after we moved in, it became clear to Fred and me that, at some point, a married couple's reproductive timetable becomes fair game for public discussion. Oddly enough, people you know as well as complete strangers feel free to weigh in on intensely private subjects such as birth control and ovulation.

I thought biological clocks only ticked internally. That's not the case. Friends, family, and society at large has its own Big "Baby" Ben. It starts ticking down the minute a couple says "I do." Before the honeymoon is over, people only hint at family expansion. Once a house is purchased, however, that whole process goes into overdrive. Phrases such as "Are you ready to start a family?" or "Is there any news you want to share with us (wink wink)?" pop up in conversation unannounced. To Fred and I, they were as uninvited as a drunk cousin at a dry wedding.

These phrases make the erroneous leap that everyone in the universe feels the need to breed. I racked my brain trying to understand why this might be true. All I could come up with were these three practical reasons couples might have for reproducing.

1) To ensure your genetic perpetuation (Considering Fred and the phlegm incident, this was not necessarily a bonus to the population at large,).

2) To have someone who feels morally obligated to take care of you when you're old and incontinent, assuming your kids like you enough to change your piddle pad on a regular basis. (If you don't play your cards right, you could end up backstroking in your own pee.)

3) To be able to stock your fireplace mantel with rows and rows of Kodak moments designed to make your family look way happier than they are in real life. The downside is that picture frames require frequent dusting (a definite drawback).

Luckily for me, I was content to live my last dribbling days in a nursing home with a dusty mantel and only a Polaroid or two of the dogs. The dogs were cuter than most babies I'd seen anyhow and were never going to require expensive college tuition. I was convinced we should leave well enough alone.

Well-meaning folks offered plenty of advice on starting a family. I listened politely, but it went in one ear and out the other. I had learned by now that if I even remotely hinted at not being ready for kids, I was bound to hear another rousing cheer of "Honey, you're NEVER ready for kids!"

The truth was, if I got too far into that conversation, I might accidentally disclose my diaper pail full of emotional insecurities. I was insecure as to what I would be like as a mother. What happened if I screwed the whole thing up? It's possible, you know. I could just see myself making my kids dislike me so much they refused to pluck my chin hairs or touch up my roots in the nursing home. I couldn't think of anything worse. It might also lead to a full disclosure of my sketchy Red Cross babysitting resume, which, if it ever got back to the Red Cross, could result in the revocation of my laminated card, something I just could not bear.

Grandparenthood was an even bigger mystery to me than parenthood. It seemed downright counterintuitive. Just when you get your life back from raising your own brood, you beg your children to take it away again with a bunch of mini-thems. I should think the empty nest would be a welcome relief from all the years of chaotic childrearing. Finally, a chance to go on a decade-long cruise and relax without anyone whining in your ear or waiting for a phone call from the police asking you to post bail. Ahhh. What a relief.

Then you foolishly go and ruin it all by encouraging your children to have children of their own. Wasn't two decades of selfless devotion enough? Grandparents should be arrested for disturbing the peace, their own peace. They should be held without bail by reason of insanity.

Inevitably, if you live in the same town as your grandchildren, free babysitting will be expected (unless you are Red Cross certified, then you should be paid, naturally). During the babysitting free-for-all, there's a good chance you'll get roped into doing the grandchildren's laundry. That is where I draw the line. Folding underwear for your own offspring is one thing, but folding underwear for your children's children who now share DNA with people who are not in your direct lineage is another thing entirely. Such madness begs the question: how far removed from the family tree does one have to be to get out of doing other people's laundry?

I don't remember my mother-in-law ever offering to fold laundry, but she was anxious to have grandchildren alright. She brought it up every chance she could. I never said it out loud; but inwardly I decided that if we ever did provide her with a grandchild, I was going to have to resist the urge to ask her to step out of the hospital room so we could have a picture of "just our family."

I didn't discuss any of this with my mom. The pen-is incident was still fresh in my mind (18 years later), an embarrassing episode we silently agreed to forget. I didn't want to ask my grandmother about having babies either, just in case she was President of the Less-Yankees-Is-More Club.

Most of my friends were married, but only a few had kids. I wondered if I was the only one who had all these questions and insecurities about mother-hood. No one really talked about it. I knew a few gals who proclaimed a desire to have children all their lives, and I was thrilled to death for them when they did. For those of us who had not, however, it seem-ed somehow less acceptable to say that out loud.

I desperately wished I could have confided my concerns to an older, wiser woman from church, but I didn't. Bible verses about being fruitful and multiplying kept floating through my head (they are pretty close to the pen-is verse, if I remember correctly), so I felt I couldn't support my hesitant position with Scripture. As far as I could tell, there weren't any Bible verses that sanctioned a personal disgust for little children, even if they whined like a banshee. The Proverbs 31 woman (a Biblical Barbie of sorts) did not blow her cool while answering a toddler's mind-numbing questions all day, even though she had to be exhausted from staying up so late and getting up at the crack of dawn. On the other hand, if I had servants to do all my house**work** and yard **work**, like she did, I might not be as ambivalent toward baby **work** in the first place.

Either way, I decided to keep my thoughts to myself. Judging by the overcrowded church nursery, there were already plenty of fruity multipliers to pass on the Faith, so I didn't feel a pressing need to contribute.

Is there a point in every woman's life where jumping into the abyss of motherhood was attractive, or at the very least, moderately inviting? There had to be. Almost every woman I knew had jumped at some point or another.

One thing was certain. I wasn't going to jump just because everyone else did. As a kid, my mother repeatedly said, "If everyone jumps off a bridge, does that mean you should jump too?" Of course not, and I was sticking to that logic, at least when it came to this subject.

Besides, having a child is not something you should "just do" because everyone else does, even if Nike recommends it. Motherhood is a huge step with lifelong ramifications. It's like bridge jumping, but without a bungee cord and a just-kidding-you-didn't-really-hit-the-bottom escape clause. Once you jump, there's no coming back.

Fred and I couldn't see why everyone was so anxious to jump in the first place. Money was Fred's main concern, and laundry was mine (among other things). By all accounts, children came out of the womb reaching for your wallet. Fred said we wouldn't be ready for that any time soon, since there was nothing to reach for yet. When it came to laundry, I hated doing my own, so washing mountains of bibs and socks, none of which belonged to me personally, was anything but inviting.

Childbirth itself was another drawback. To say that I was a little concerned about the process of squeezing a small person roughly the size of a Cabbage Patch Doll through a canal the width of a cheese stick would be an understatement.

Getting to the squeezing point was another issue entirely. I used to think pregnancy only affected your tummy. (Undoubtedly, this was another unrealistic expectation produced by watching too many prosthetic bellies on television.) I'd overheard plenty of conversations between my nursing coworkers, most of whom were moms. The graphic terms they used made it crystal clear pregnancy was much more involved than the emergence of a darling little "baby bump."

I was familiar with the concepts of stretch marks, hemorrhoids, and varicose veins from nursing school but that was a sterilized version (no pun intended). Listening to real women describe their demise firsthand was completely different, and downright frightening. Who knew there were body parts one could shove back in, tuck back up, tie in knots, or do without altogether? I couldn't see a single "pro" in prolapse at this point. One needn't be particularly vain to shudder at words like sagging, bloating, bulging, and drooping. I wasn't particularly happy with the figure I was bringing to the delivery table in the first place, and by all accounts the one I would leave with was worse.

Of course, there are always exceptions to the baby-figure-wrecking rule, though I doubted I would be one of them. Hollywood starlets are in that category. Those gals are cinematic freaks of nature, able to squeeze into a designer gown just moments after birth. Supermodels are equally mystifying, able to jump off the delivery table and back into haute couture by the time their milk comes in. Female Olympians have that anatomical knack as well, competing to get back into their skinny jeans before Bob Costas can say "Apgar."

I had a friend who had that physical "gift." She wanted me to film the birth of her third child, saying she would call me in plenty of time to capture "the crowning moment" (which, unfortunately, had nothing to do with tiaras). Thirty minutes after she called, I ran in the door to her hospital room, huffing and puffing from my sprint across the parking lot. I expected to see her with her legs up in stirrups, grunting like a Hungarian dead-lifter. She was nowhere to be seen.

I worried, thinking she had been wheeled out for an emergency C-section or worse. Just as I started to leave, she yoo-hooed to me from the bathroom, informing me that Baby #3 had made a quick appearance and all was well down under. I missed the whole thing. The baby was already in the nursery and she was in the bathroom "freshening up," look-ing like someone who'd had a hard day at the mall rather than a woman who'd just dropped a placenta out of her nether regions. Disgusted, I couldn't help but notice she even had on matching earrings and a bracelet, something I only do when I am going out for my anniversary.

From that moment on, I decided women like her were leftover relics, throwbacks from the days when popping out a baby in the field was the norm. It was a genetic predisposition, and there was no doubt in my mind I was at the shallow end of that gene pool.

So, given the laundry, the monetary drain, and the potential for anatomical destruction, I had to wonder, "What is the payoff for having kids?" Babies are cute but given the cost (on so many levels), cute is simply not enough. In other words, if there truly *was* some sort of invisible jumping-off point into parenthood, I was going to need more than a little push. I was going to need a good old-fashioned foot-to-the-back shove.

A couple of years later, during a party celebrating Fred's Master's degree, my sister-in-law pulled me aside to ask if this milestone meant we would be "starting our family" now. I didn't like that phrase or its implication, and quite frankly, I was tired of hearing it.

What did she mean by that? Fred and I *were* a family. Our dogs were our family. Our friends were family. Why did everyone assume that children were the only way a couple could start a family? Thoughtlessly, I blurted out, "No, we are not interested, not thinking about it, complete *as is,* blah, blah, blah," as if it were a crime to have asked the question.

"Why do you ask?" I snapped, in defense mode.

She smiled and said gently, "Because we are. I am excited to say, I am due in April" in a thrilled-to-be-expecting-so-please-be-happy-for-us voice. Her words came as a shock, like an emotional taser to the heart. It took less than a split second for me to determine that this was not the correct timeline of events.

"What? How dare they?" I thought to myself. "We were married first! By two years! Fred is the firstborn! He's the future Patriarch! I'm the Princess Diana, and she's the Duchess of York! I'm supposed to have the heir, she can have the spare!" My mind reeled at the incredulous usurping of our right to bear the first grandchild.

Didn't she know there was a proper way to do things? There *had* to be a rulebook somewhere containing a checklist of prerequisites for "starting a family." Surely birth order was at the top of that list. It didn't matter that we didn't *want* children at the moment. What mattered was that we were checking boxes, and they checked the baby box before we checked ours. That was not the proper order of events. At least, in *my* mind.

I began to go over the checklist I kept in my head. Fred and I had been married for several years. Check. Between the two of us we had degrees, jobs, cars, and a home with central heat and air. Check. We had every possible form of insurance and a small savings account. We paid our bills on time, changed our oil every 3000 miles, and got our teeth cleaned twice a year. Check, check, check. We had a fenced-in yard with two dogs, both of which were distempered, dewormed, and desexed. We had a safety deposit box, paid our taxes on time, and cleaned up after our pets in public. Over-check. We owned a lawn mower, a rake, and a few plumbing tools. Irrelevant, but I checked it anyways. We read the Bible, the paper, and

Consumer Reports, though not always in that order. We were responsible and independent. What else was needed before bringing a child into the world?

I sincerely wanted to be happy for my sister-in-law, but congratulations are hard to squeeze out of a jealous heart. I wasn't jealous of her pregnancy but of her *confidence* about becoming pregnant and being a mother.

She had always talked about having children, and I knew she was going to make one heck of a mom. I found it hard to be supportive when I wasn't sure I was ever going to be a good fit for motherhood. That was the one box I wasn't sure I could check, and it was the most important box of all.

Deep down, I knew there were more important prerequisites for parenting than mortgages and diplomas. I knew important virtues like patience and kindness played a big role in dealing with children, something I wasn't entirely sure I possessed. I always admired how Ma Ingalls dealt with Laura, even when she did something really stupid. (That whiny Nellie Olson was usually to blame in the end, proving once again that whining is the root of all evil). I only hoped that if, and when, I jumped the invisible precipice, I would be like my lovely sister-in-law, happy and glowing with the joyous anticipation of motherhood.

Within months, it seemed as though everywhere I looked, someone was pregnant. I couldn't go anywhere without bumping into a protruding belly or double stroller. Even the mall I frequented was suddenly overflowing with maternity shops and baby items. Dozens of television commercials featured adorable talking babies, which led me to wonder, "Was it always like this, or did this phenomenon occur overnight?" I was a bit perturbed by its all-consuming prevalence.

Not long after that, I found myself in an unfamiliar aisle in the grocery store. Somehow I had drifted into the baby food aisle by mistake. While scanning for a quick emergency exit, my eye caught a glimpse of a tiny jar of applesauce with a picture of a chubby little baby on it.

That angelic face stared right into my soul. I tried to look away but those long eyelashes followed me, like a baby Mona Lisa. "How adorable," I said to myself. "How insane," I answered back as I carefully picked up the jar. The fact that this conversation went back and forth for a few seconds should have made me put Baby Mona back on the shelf and call an intervention on myself. Instead, I bought the jar and hid it in the back of our kitchen cabinets as if to silence the beckoning baby.

Toward the end of the summer, I fainted, presumably from the intense summer heat. As I came to, I heard someone say, "I'll bet she's pregnant." Bite your tongue, I thought, as the words sunk in quickly. Could it be true? Had I finally fallen off the precipice, or did someone shove me when I wasn't looking? My eyes rolled back in my head. Darn it, I knew I shouldn't have bought that applesauce.*

* Note to self: Gerber is not a brand of birth control.

Chapter 12

The ~~Dead~~ Rabbit is Right on Target

"You know what your problem is, it's that you haven't seen enough movies. All of life's riddles are answered in the movies."
Steve Martin

I mentioned the fainting incident to a coworker, who proceeded to grin from ear to ear. Seriously, she seemed waaay happier about it than I was. She was the mother of three and working on number four (if I overheard correctly). Her face lit up like a power plant at the mere mention of her children, something I had a hard time understanding since she confessed that the only way she could polish her fingernails was to strap her kids in the minivan, slap on a coat of polish, and drive. She went on to say that if she was lucky, she could apply two coats before reaching her destination, applying a quick-dry sealer between stoplights. (And cell phones are a distraction?)   Using only her palms, she had mastered the art of angling the air vents toward the steering wheel for maximum drying time lest she smudge the paint job while unbuckling her bambinos. "That's no way to live!" I thought, as I tried to envision her manipulating the vents with stiff Frankenstein hands.   Her goofy grin must be a result of all the fumes generated in an enclosed space, I surmised, and nothing more.   A true friend would never wish that lifestyle on her worst enemy, much less someone she liked.

Still grinning, Nurse Top Coat suggested I send a urine sample to the lab for a pregnancy test. "I'd be more than happy to take it for you!" she cooed.   Her enthusiasm was beginning to irritate me.   I acquiesced, wondering if the old-fashioned inject-a-rabbit-and-see-if-it-dies test was still the medical protocol for confirming a pregnancy like in my mom's day.   The more I thought about it, I realized PETA would never stand for that.   I could just imagine a laboratory full of adorable caged bunnies being set free by zealous animal rights protestors.

"What a wonderful surprise this would be!" my friend exclaimed as she ran out the door holding the still-warm specimen cup up in the air like an Olympic torch.   Surprise was not the word I would have used in this instance.

First of all, I had been married for several years.

With that comes the statistical possibility of parenthood and with Fred, the statistics were high. You don't have to be a rocket scientist (like Fred) to figure out what I mean by that.

We used birth control (something crazy fertile talk show guests desperately need a tutorial on). But as "they" say, nothing is fool proof. My dad always said there was only one reliable method of birth control: aspirin. "Put one between your knees and hold it there," he would say. In other words, I was long past the days of being legitimately "surprised" by pregnancy.

Secondly, I always thought of surprises as something pleasant and fun, like a surprise birthday party, or a surprise visit from an old friend. The word "surprise" was full of positive connotations, at least in my mind. A surprise was when something unexpectedly fabulous happened to you, like winning a Ferrari or a trip to Italy. If those were suddenly bestowed upon you, you would classify it as a great surprise indeed.

On the other hand, if someone unexpectedly gave you a Pinto or a one-way bus ticket to Detroit, you might be a little less than thrilled, labeling that as more of a disaster than a surprise. To me, a "surprise baby" fell into that category. It was practically an oxymoron.

As my shift came a close, the Ovarian Fairy returned. Quickly, she grabbed my arm and looked both ways before pulling me into the linen vestibule as though we were top-secret spies flying under the radar.

Her eyes were practically fluorescent as she silently mouthed the words "It's positive!" As stealthily as she pulled me in, she whizzed out to perform life-saving CPR, something I thought I might need myself in a few minutes.

I wanted to go home and hide under the covers, so I jumped in to my VW Rabbit. I loved my little diesel Rabbit. My dad had purchased a dark brown Rabbit for himself and then a white model for my mother. Shortly thereafter, they bought a tan version, which made it look as though our Rabbits had been cross-bred in the garage like, well, rabbits. At that particular moment, I felt a bit like a rabbit myself, desperately hoping there was only one little bunny in my personal garage rather than an entire litter.

As if on autopilot, my trusty 2-door steered me straight to the nearest Target. This was a strange detour. I had not felt the need to go to Target before I was with child. Well, that's not exactly true. I always felt the need to go to Target. I loved the Big Red Bullseye and would worship, er, shop there three times a day if I could, like a retail Mecca. If you've ever been there, you know what I'm talking about. On any given day, it's possible to innocently enter through the red double doors looking for a ten dollar item you actually *need*, and end up checking out with an extra eighty dollars of stuff you simply *must have*.* No one could fault you.

---

* A phenomenon known as impulse buying. This was my husband's major complaint about my budgeting, or lack thereof. Fred and I were watching our pennies (since pennies were all we had), so I stayed out of Target like drunks stay out of bars. (For the most part.)

Everything in Target is so incredibly inviting it practically jumps in your cart while you're not looking.

All that being said, this wasn't a typical jaunt to Target, especially for me. If this were just one day before, I would have grabbed my big red cart and headed straight to the shoe section. Next, I would have casually sashayed to the circular of sunglasses, giving it a twirl, and trying on a pair or two for size.

Next, I would have glanced over the scarves and purses before checking out the new arrivals at the jewelry counter. I might have even stocked up on toiletries or ventured to the home goods department, wondering which item I could beg Fred to sanction next month. I would wrap up the shopping excursion by perusing the make-up aisle, acquiring a new tube of lip-gloss or sparkly eye shadow of which I had no real need. That was yesterday.

Today's visit was more like an unconscious foraging for emotional comfort food. Target just happened to be my restaurant of choice. It was the retail equivalent of mashed potatoes or macaroni and cheese. Today, I felt more like an alien, sent on a very specific mission; a mission from The Hormonal Mother Ship.

In an effort to complete said mission, my lunar buggy dragged me to the active wear department, a section I rarely visited. In front of me stood a circular rack of women's fleece wear in a variety of girlish colors.

As if in a trance, I grabbed an oversized pink sweat-shirt and matching pink sweatpants and tossed them into the cart.

Clearly, I wasn't myself. I didn't even bother to try the sweatpants on, a shopping faux pas reserved for amateurs and stick thin women who can actually fit into garments labeled "one size fits all."*

This was an impulse buy if ever there was one. Even though the garments were on sale, Fred would balk at my purchase if he were there. Sale prices did not impress Fred in the least. He only cared "if we could afford it in the first place." It's hard to believe he is even an American.

I had no idea what could possibly have trigger-ed this mindless purchase of pastel fleece wear in the heat of August. Perhaps an emergency message had been sent directly to the weight-gain-alert center of my brain, suggesting that ten minutes into gestation, I needed to buy elasticized balloon-wear big enough for two.

After all, I *would* need something comfor-table to wallow around in for the next eight months while my body went to pot. I was keenly aware that pregnancy was often a trigger for the phenomenon my parents frequently referred to as "letting yourself go." I wasn't exactly sure what that meant, but I could

---

* *I don't know who "All" is, but she and I have vastly different measurements.*

tell by the way they said it that it wasn't a glowing compliment. I had horrific visions of Svelte Barbie becoming Biggest Loser Barbie in nine short months. What was next? Bag Lady Barbie? She couldn't be far behind. (Pigeons sold separately.) Was that the inevitable progression when a woman had a baby? I was afraid to find out.

Later that evening, I decided to tell Fred "the news." Due to our history of ambiguity, I wasn't sure what he would say when he heard that we were having a baby. As soon as I uttered "the news," I watched as the idea ricocheted around in his brain, pinging between his cerebrum and cerebellum a few times before it finally hit him square between the eyes. It was like watching a pinball machine, waiting for the final score to light up his face and tell me if I was a winner or not. I held my breath, naively hoping that the romantic soap opera version would unfold.

You know what I'm talking about. We've all seen it a thousand times in movies and on television. The beautiful young wife quietly announces to her studly husband that she is indeed carrying his child. With over-the-moon delight (every Hollywood couple's nauseating cliché), the dashing young husband smiles uncontrollably, thrilled at the thought of becoming a father with the woman of his dreams. In a grand and affectionate gesture, he sweeps her off her feet, literally, all the while insisting that his lovely bride "take it easy" until the blessed event.

"Don't move a muscle," he would instruct with rugged authority, as if protecting a glass figurine that might accidentally break.

"Don't be silly," she would protest, trying to conceal her elated reaction to his protective mandate. When she tries to explain, the dashing father-to-be gently shushes her by placing his fingertips to her lips. She acquiesces, all the while smiling on the inside. He is her Prince Charming, and with this pregnancy, she has successfully secured her title as Queen of His Heart forever. Yes, I had seen the scene a thousand times and waited for it to happen to me.

"Snap out of it, Sal," Fred said as he summoned me out of my delusion with a quick snap of his fingers. He had just finished saying that while of course he was happy with "the news," this also meant our time as a twosome was coming to a close, which made him a bit melancholy. His little sister was eleven years younger than him, so the memory of diapers, crying, and babysitting was still fresh. To my dismay, that is where his mind had dropped anchor.

No swooning. No sweeping. No shushing. He might as well have pulled out a piece of graph paper and used his mechanical pencil to draw an algorithm of how the arrival of a child would diminish our lives to diapers, debt, and doldrums within a few short years.

Have you noticed that soap opera characters are never engineers? There's a reason for that.

In the weeks to come, the reaction from friends was about as underwhelming as Fred's. "Seriously... you're pregnant?" they pondered in disbelief, no doubt recalling my recent plans to franchise child-free restaurants. Hoping for a little more enthusiasm, we decided to share "the news" with the prospective grandparents.

My mother had just flown in for a visit, so she received the announcement in person. She was skeptical about the validity of the pregnancy since my first prenatal visit was not for another week. In her day, a suspected bun in the oven was never *officially* announced until the doctor examined the contents of the oven himself, and the rabbit turned up dead. Thankfully, that ancient practice has long since been replaced by peeing blindly on a stick to see if a plus sign appears. It's kind of messy, but at least no animals are harmed in the process.

Undeterred by my mother's reservations, Fred phoned my dad on speaker, letting him know that his first grandchild was on the way. "The news" was met with an enthusiastic round of "atta boys" and "good job Fred!" as though we had entered an Olympic sperm relay, and Fred's genetic contestants had come in just under the wire.

While I appreciated my dad's enthusiastic response, why all the "atta boys??" Making babies was not a reproductive sporting event. Even if it were, why was Fred the only one getting a pat on the back?

How come no congratulations rang out over my precision ovulation? I didn't get any high-fives for keeping the fallopian freeways clear. I didn't hear any kudos about my uterus being in pristine condition for implantation.   So why all the chauvinistic fuss over Fred's contribution? For the most part, Fred was done.

In essence, my dad was rallying around the sprinter, when the embryonic marathoner could have used a little encouragement.   After all, it was *I* who would be crossing a finish line in the delivery room 8 months from now. Fred wouldn't be the one to bloat and swell for the better part of a year, ballooning to the size of a 4-H prize heifer. *I* would. Fred wouldn't be wearing ugly smocked jumpers that could comfortably sleep six. *I* would. Fred would sleep soundly through the night while I awoke multiple times to empty my bladder. He would lie on his stomach. I would lie about my weight.

No doubt Fred would be in the delivery room when the big moment came, but when it came right down to brass tacks, he didn't *have* to be there to get the job done. I did. He could leave anytime he wanted to, and the end result would be the same. I couldn't. And yet, *he* was getting a pat on the back? Way to take one for the team, Fred.

As expected, Doctor Dead Rabbit "officially" confirmed that I had been successfully wired to explode with placental girth. During the all-important first pre-natal visit, every possible maternal subject was covered, from vitamins to stretch marks, birthing classes to scholarship applications. It was a bit overwhelming; but when I checked out at the sliding glass window, I got a little shopping bag with free samples of baby stuff, which made it feel a little like going to the mall. I'm pretty sure they plan that feel-good ending so you come back at least once before the baby's born.

During my examination, the doctor cheerfully asked if there was anything I had wanted to accomplish up to that point that I hadn't gotten around to. What kind of question is that to ask a hormonally-charged incubator? "Yes, as a matter of fact there is," I answered tersely, with an unexpected surge of brutal honesty. "I've always wanted to own a Volvo. I suppose now I never will," I said, recalling Fred's algorithm which definitely precluded the purchase of a pricey foreign car.

The doctor furrowed her brow and muttered, "Hmmm, we have a disparity here." I wondered if she thought the Volvo was too flashy, not a good *Consumer Reports* buy, or had another make and model to suggest.

Rather, my due date was the source of concern. She needed to confirm the D.O.C., or Date of Confinement. That's a horrible term. To a pregnant woman, the word "confinement" conjures up images of maternal straight jackets or prenatal life without parole. Before I could fully launch into my protest over the terminology, Dr. Due Date said she needed to perform an internal ultrasound, which sounded anything but ultra when she described what it would entail. Jokingly, I suggested she try another lucky spin with the wheel-of-fortune-thing-a-ma-gig obstetricians use to predict the due date like Nostradamus. She was not amused.

Moments later, I was riding the horizontal horsey, with my feet in metal stirrups. I was nervous, not about the procedure, but because of what I was about to see. I half-expected to see a pair of huge goo-gly eyes staring back at me through the amniotic fluid, like a big goldfish in a plastic bag of water. (I had won one at the fair as a kid, even though I had really hoped to win a stuffed animal. A small, but memorable disappointment.)

It turns out I was nervous for nothing, since the only thing revealed by the not-so-ultra-ultrasound was a tiny white speck on a fuzzy black background. Apparently, to the trained eye, this speck was in just the right place, with just the right dimensions, to be a microscopic human being. To the doctor, it looked like our future son or daughter. To us, it looked like a grain of rice. We decided to name it Uncle Ben, and the cooking timer was set for May first.

Chapter 13

Morning, ~~Noon and Night~~ Sickness

"Remember we're all in this alone."
Lily Tomlin

With gritted teeth, I clutched my purse as I hurried to the parking lot, praying that my Rabbit keys would magically appear in my hand before I got sick.

Fred had always referred to my large leather handbag as "the black hole," and for once, I understood his frustration. I'd never had any trouble finding items in my purse, at least until now. Like a hand to a cookie, I could always locate my wallet or a lipstick with a simple brush of my fingertips, a skill most women perfect by years of fumbling around in a dark purse. Today, however, my keys had a mind of their own, and I cursed the fact that Fred was right about my choice of handbags.

The next wave of nausea hit a little more forcefully than the first. A few moments earlier, I had been taken completely by surprise as a consuming wave of acid rose violently to the back of my throat. I made a beeline for the exit before the check out clerk could even utter "Have a nice day." (We all know how much that is worth anyways.) I swallowed hard, clenching my teeth together, to keep the overflow at bay. "I must be getting the flu," I thought as I quickly flung my purse in the car and headed for home, the land of milk and Tums.

Fast and furiously, I drove over the speed limit (as every good Chicagoan does), hearing the phrase "Have you had a BM today?" echo over and over in my mind in a sweet Southern drawl. I always heard my Grandmother's voice say that in my head when I started to feel sick, since her remedy for every ill was "a nice long sit on the pot." I desperately hoped Grandma's overly simplistic cure-all would work in this case but I had my doubts.

The next wave of nausea hit like a baby Tsunami. If a trip to the loo was the solution, I'd pull over this instant and find the nearest ladies room; but this was no ordinary nausea. I thought it might be car sickness, until I realized that I was sick before I got in the car. Oh no. That wasn't a good sign.

As I drove, I tried to calculate how far along I was. I counted backwards to my fainting incident, and then counted forward, adding the days in my head. I squinted, hoping it would help me see the invisible numbers as I carried the 2 to the tens column in the air with my finger. I reassured myself that morning sickness couldn't possibly be the culprit for this misery. Based on my mental calculations, morning sickness should have reared its ugly head weeks ago. Could it be that math was not my strong suit as well? No one had ever accused me of being a mathematical savant, but this was simple addition for crying out loud. How many academic cracks can one student fall through?

A swift mental refresher course on my maternity nursing material reassured me that math wasn't the *real* issue after all. I had forgotten that morning sickness didn't begin the moment an egg and sperm collide. Why had I assumed it did? Perhaps because TV's portrayal of pregnancy made it appear that way. In Hollywood, the moment a baby is conceived there is an immediate chain reaction starting with the fallopian "red phone." Sensing the presence of a fertilized egg, the Fallophone dialed up the mother's gut relaying an immediate signal to go ahead and retch. I'd seen the same predictable scenario over and over. Just as a woman announces she is expecting a baby, she claps her hand over her mouth and races toward the toilet where, it's safe to say, she is *not* going to have a BM. "Another stupid TV myth debunked," I thought as I was rudely interrupted by an uncontrollable urge to pull over and spill my stomach contents onto the side of the road.

Morning sickness is the biggest misnomer in the galaxy. Whoever named it did not have my version of it. I wasn't just sick in the morning. That I could have handled. Rather, I was sick all morning, for most of the afternoon, *and* well into the evening. In other words, from the time I got up until the time my head hit the pillow I was queasy beyond belief. There were only one or two hours in the middle of each day when I did not feel as though I had been on a Tilt-a-Whirl far longer than a human being was meant to be.

The technical name for this severe morning sickness is Hyperemesis Gravidarum, or HG for short. It is fairly uncommon, and often misunderstood. So much so that until Kate Middleton suffered from it, very few people had any knowledge of the condition. Only folks who live under a rock wouldn't recognize that name. In case you are one of them, Kate is married to Prince William, the eldest son of the late Princess Diana. (Crawl on out. It's beautiful up here.) The lovely, young Duchess was hospitalized with the condition, as it usually results in severe dehydration. I felt her pain. I guess it's just something us Royals are cursed with.

Suffice it to say, equating typical morning sickness to HG is like equating a broken leg to being a quadriplegic. There is no comparison. Neither is desirable, but one is manageable. The other is incapacitating.

The only food I could keep down was cherry Pop Tarts. If the kid ever broke a bone, cherry filling was going to ooze out. Sometimes I could keep down Chinese food but it always resurfaced right before bed.

Night after night my fortune read, "Be careful what you eat; Chinese food come back to haunt you in middle of night."

Plenty of mommy-to-be literature addressed the subject of nausea, just not *this kind of nausea.* This was not typical run-of-the-mill first trimester queasiness. I looked for answers but they eluded me. There was no internet to search, no Google to scour, and no Web doctor to consult. I had to rely solely on books for information, and they were as helpful as a hairnet on a bald man. In fact, one very popular prenatal book had the gall to suggest that women who reported severe morning sickness were simply in need of a little extra TLC rather than true medical attention. Fred wanted to burn that book, a truly romantic gesture in my eyes.

I had thrown up before, but not like this. This was more of an eruption, a violent upheaval that burst the tiny blood vessels in my eyes. The result was highly unattractive, if not downright scary. I looked like I had been on a month-long crying jag. My freakish appearance precipitated substantial alarm in adults, as well as a gasp of horror in small children. Why Lord? Why me? Some women glowed when they were pregnant. The only glow I had was from toilet water splashing back onto my swollen, bloodshot face. I felt miserable, and it showed.

To make matters worse, every time I got sick, I wet myself uncontrollably. I thought I had 50 years or so before I encountered the delights of incontinence, but I was wrong. It seemed inconceivable that something the size of a Jolly Rancher could exert enough force on a human bladder to make it burst like a water balloon, but it did. (I wonder if my buddy Kate, the future Queen of England, leaked royally as well.) Something as simple as a trip to the grocery store became an instant disaster if I failed to make it to the ladies room in time. I could only assume that bathroom placement was the product of male engineering. They were *always* in the farthest corner from where I was.

This added complication made it impossible to continue working. Certain sights, smells, and sounds common to working in a hospital precipitated an unexpected gastric upheaval followed by a tidal wave down south. It simply wasn't cool (or entirely ethical) to leave critical patients unattended, so a leave of absence became necessary.

Staying home drove me crazy. I didn't know what to do with myself. I was a do-er, not a sitter (unless children were involved, and even then, I wasn't good at it). My day consisted of getting up, eating, getting sick, changing my clothes, laying down, eating, getting sick,… well, you get the picture. I just wanted to go back to work. Even "people-pleasing" was better than this.

Not only was pregnancy taking a toll on my body, it was robbing me of my IQ as well. One day, I tried to withdraw money from an ATM machine; but it kept spitting my bankcard back at me. After a third frustrating attempt, the gentleman in line behind me kindly pointed out that I had been using my library card. Perhaps it was best that I was done administering narcotics, at least for the time being.

As the weeks dragged on, Fred and I listened to well-meaning anecdotes concerning my "condition." Together, we endured countless questions such as "Have you tried saltines?" Outwardly, I smiled. Through bloodshot eyes I politely responded, "Saltines? What a great idea! I'll have to try that." Inside, I seethed at the simplicity of the suggestion. I wanted to smack my forehead (and the person) and yell, "Saltines! Wow! If only I had thought of that!" with the same dumb-founded expression as the guy who "coulda had a V-8!"

Of course we had tried saltines! We weren't complete idiots. That would be like asking a migraine sufferer if they'd given aspirin a whirl. What a ridiculous thing to say to someone who was carrying airplane sickness bags on them at all times. I had not only tried saltines, I had tried soup, ginger-ale, ginger root, and sips of flat gingerized Cola. I tried acupressure, aroma-therapy, and mind-bending visualization, all without success. I even tried cruise-ship wristbands that promised to help me sail through morning sickness like a breeze, but they turned out to be as helpful as a paddle on the Titanic.

Fred always nodded in solidarity during these interrogations, reassuring folks that we would try everything they suggested. It was sweet of him to speak on my behalf; but after twenty weeks of hearing him discuss how sick "we" were, I had to object.

I understood that when men use the term "we" in regards to pregnancy ("We are pregnant!", or "We are going to have natural childbirth."), it is with the best of intentions. In fact, it's almost cute. I'll admit, the terminology is endearing but it is miles away from the truth.

Why do people accept that terminology when it comes to having a baby? No one has ever said "we" are having a root canal, or "we" are the President of the United States. It's simply not possible. Oh, the Vice President may be asked to chime in now and then but inevitably the buck stops with the President. Period. And your significant other can accompany you to your procedure, but in the end, the drill goes in one mouth and one mouth only, no matter how hard they squeeze your hand for support. So, whether you're in the dental office or the Oval Office, there is only one chair and only one person can sit in it at a time. By definition, some experiences simply cannot be shared. Morning sickness was one of them.

Don't get me wrong. Fred would have shouldered the burden if he could have. Even though it was my head in the toilet, watching me endure this misery was its own form of torture for Fred. He knew this was not merely a temporary deficit of TLC. Nor was this a case of gee-she-is-pregnant-so-let's-give-her-a-back-rub-and-everything-will-be-better-hysteria. He knew better. Poor Fred had witnessed two trimesters of straight up day-in-day-out-get-me-off-this-roller-coaster-or-I'll-scream nausea and vomiting, and he had no clue how to make it stop.

When the nausea threatened my health, Doctor Stork prescribed anti-nausea medication as a last resort. It made me sleepy and unable to do much more than lay on my side all day like a slug. I was disappointed in my pathetic ability to be pregnant and be productive at the same time.

Unfortunately, I had hour upon hour to ponder my situation. I began to feel sorry for myself, and ask what the heck happened to me? How did I become the care receiver, rather than the care giver? I hated that even more than I hated being a "people-person." What happened to the go-getter I used to be? Where was the self-sufficient girl who loved to sing, wallpaper 'til midnight, and work twelve hours straight with energy to spare. I wanted her back.

What was wrong with me anyhow? Why was I so sick, while other women sailed through pregnancy without a hitch? Was it genetics? Nutrition? Relative position to the equator? I went through every possible scenario and came up empty. In my mother's day, pregnant women smoked cigarettes and drank martinis.

They even took diet pills to stay cocktail-dress-ready and never had a bit of trouble. I had done everything by the book and look where it had gotten me.

The inability to earn a paycheck combined with a complete lack of energy drained away every ounce of confidence I'd ever had, dragging my self-esteem down the drain with it. I hated feeling helpless. If only I could find a set of bootstraps with which I could pull myself up by, I would do it in a heartbeat, but they were nowhere to be found.

I didn't want to share any of these thoughts with other people because I didn't want them to think less of me. So I cried out to God instead. Perhaps I had done something to deserve this, something awful that I couldn't even remember! Had I made God angry? Was this some sort of punishment? Was God disappointed in me, sighing and grumbling under His breath about my lack of stick-to-it-iveness or self-discipline? I had hoped He wasn't, but I had no plausible explanation for this affliction and no frame of reference for a Father, other than a disgruntled one.

Maybe the restaurant idea was coming back to haunt me. I guess I should have kept that under wraps, just like my unintelligent giggling. Perhaps if I had been a kinder, gentler babysitter, more of a people-person, less mouthy (the list went on and on), I wouldn't be sick all day. The number of times these thoughts went round and around in my head was enough to make anyone throw up.

"Was this because of my ambivalence toward motherhood?" I uttered in shameful silence to God and myself. I wanted God to know that I loved Uncle Ben with all my heart, but I was still so unsure about what kind of mother I would be. I wanted to be a good mom (who doesn't?), but I couldn't see past my shortcomings, and I was scared to let anyone see that.

At least I was honest with God, something I hoped He could appreciate since honesty was His idea in the first place. I knew in my head that God so loved the world, even when we were in a pitiful state, but I seriously doubted in my heart that He could tolerate this pathetic, unproductive version of me for very long. I knew I couldn't.

I wished like crazy that Fred didn't have to see me like this. I cringed at the thought of how he must view his blushing, red-eyed bride now that the honeymoon was definitely over. I felt fat, ugly, and useless. I half expected Fred to call it quits and hit the door. After all, having a wife that wets herself five times a day definitely qualifies as "letting yourself go."

Rather than rejecting me, Fred came home every day on his lunch hour to check on me. He spoke with sympathy about my discomfort and told me how sorry he was that I was miserable. He never once complained about the messy house, the Chinese carry out, or my drowsy state of mind. He told me he loved me every day, and even called me beautiful, a real leap of faith when your wife is swimming in her own drool.

Fred's unexpected compassion kept me going. I also read a daily Psalm to keep my spirits up. When I got to Psalm 119: 71, I read these words: "My suffering was good for me, for it taught me to pay attention to your decrees" (NLT). I caught my breath. Pay attention to your decrees. That's what it said. The first decree that popped into my head was "love is patient, love is kind" from I Corinthians 13, the famous love chapter.

In that one instant, my whole ordeal made sense.

My suffering wasn't a punishment or a curse from God. It wasn't even a problem for that matter. Rather, it was in fact, a gift. A gift I didn't even know I needed, from a loving God who knew exactly what I needed to prepare me for what lay ahead.

In that moment, I realized that neediness was not a crime. Rather, it was a condition - the human condition, and I was experiencing it like I never had before. My neediness was not something I could help, and was in no way cause for guilt or shame. All the work ethic and self-sufficiency I could muster wasn't going to change my body's reaction to pregnancy, and I had a choice whether to wallow in my disappointment, or learn from it.

I learned that the suffering I had endured was not because I was unloved, but rather, because I *was*.

Once I embraced that fact, my eyes were opened to another truth, one I desperately needed to see. God knew that in just a few short months, I was going to care for a baby, the neediest of all creatures. Newborns are the complete opposite of self-sufficient beings, because they rely on the mercy of others for even their most basic needs. They can't feed themselves, they can't earn money, and they can't get ready in ten minutes or less. They have no baby bootstraps to pull themselves up by, and even if they did, they would need assistance to do it. Infants are simply small versions of regular people, except that they are unable to care for themselves, a trait I would have despised just a few months earlier.

Even though babies are not self-sufficient in the least, they are created by God, and therefore have intrinsic value. They may cry, drool, and pee all over themselves (something I had a new appreciation for), yet are still deserving of love, respect, and dignity.

In His wisdom, God allowed me to feel as helpless as the infant I was carrying, in order to help me be the mother I so desperately wanted to be. It taught me His decrees; patience, kindness, and empathy for the weak.

He also knew that it was the only way I could ever fully understand that my value as a person had absolutely *nothing* to do with my ability to be self-sufficient, and *everything* to do with being created in His image.

Something else clicked during those long dreary months. I realized that while Fred's wardrobe may not have been ready for the cover of GQ, he had so many wonderful qualities; qualities that are much harder to find in a mate, and way more important than appearance could ever be. It turned out that my Fred was not a "fixer-upper" after all, at least in ways that mattered most.

I guess "we" were really pregnant after all. I was sick with gratitude.

Chapter 14

Weighing in
on the ~~New Dieting~~ Rules

*"A lot of people are afraid of heights. Not me.
I'm afraid of widths."*
Steven Wright

I had no idea there were so many rules during pregnancy. (In fact, if there was anything in life that *didn't* come with rules, I had yet to see it.) From the get-go, I was told that hair dye, kitty litter, and raw meat are serious offenders on the maternity hit list. That I could handle. In addition, I was to avoid harsh fumes, artificial sweeteners, electric blankets, and MSG. Totally doable since my internal thermostat was set on inferno, and pop-tarts don't contain MSG. I'm glad someone shared that information with me because up to that point all I knew was that roller coasters were inadvisable (I could read the signs like anybody else), and boarding a transcontinental flight to Australia once your contractions had begun was a rather bad idea.

It was hard to decide what was a real danger and what wasn't. There was a lot of misinformation out there about neo-natal threats, and the whole thing got a little scary. Everything from liquid paper to paper towels appeared to be a threat to fertile women. Someone (who will remain nameless, but their middle name is "they") even suggested that eating peanut butter can cause brain damage. I knew that had to be a lie or the whole nation would be sitting in an institution eating Reese's Peanut Butter Cups. No matter how ridiculous such warnings were, it was easy to become alarmed, especially when my hormones were raging out of control.

As a result, I became suspicious of everything. I felt like I should avoid hair dryers, remote controls and controlling people. I started to be fearful of lunar eclipses, full moons, crescent moons, crescent rolls, and movies that featured vampires that howl at the moon (ours weren't cute and sparkly yet, remember?).

In hopes of securing a genetically intact reproduction, I steered clear of the aforementioned dangers, and just to be on the safe side, I stayed away from any other questionable DNA-damagers such as glass cleaner, furniture polish, and dishwashing liquid. I threw in every type of housekeeping agent for good measure, including laundry detergent and scented dryer sheets. I didn't know if those were genuine embryonic no-no's, but I wasn't going to take any chances. I cataloged and eliminated all conceivable chromosomal threats, including the potentially dangerous acts of grocery shopping and laundry. By no means was I going to invite a plethora of potential birth defects generated by overcrowded checkout lanes or strenuous sock matching.

It's a wonder that child-bearing females don't just hole up in an obstetrician-approved bunker during their reproductive years. When, and only when they've popped out their entire collection of offspring, should they re-emerge into the pregnancy danger zone we call Planet Earth. I didn't want to screw Uncle Ben up even before he arrived.

By the beginning of my third trimester, I had gained only eight pounds. Every ounce of it was in my upper body. Ten minutes after the rabbit died, I was in a Z cup, and an additional growth spurt had occurred. Thing 3 and Thing 4 sprouted under my armpits like dairy reservoirs ready to explode. It was as though my lactation ducts had been enlarged and remodeled in anticipation of feeding a small country. I've seen women who carry their babies like a little round basketball tucked under their shirt. From the backside, they don't even look pregnant. That wasn't me. As much as I knew I should, it's hard to love those lucky gals when your breasts are the width of a cruise ship and even your earrings don't fit anymore.

Eight pounds was nothing for me, actually. I could rack that up over a holiday or a weekend of heavy babysitting. It was less than normal for a woman at my stage of pregnancy, but the doctor reassured me the baby was getting all the nourishment it needed from my maternal "stores." I pictured Uncle Ben going up and down the aisles of my stomach, putting little calcium blocks into his prenatal shopping cart.

I cannot remember a time in my life when weight wasn't an issue. I was not overweight, but I was not skinny either; and in my mind, skinny was "good." In fact, the skinnier, the better. Everyone on TV was skinny. So was my best friend. She was short and petite, something I was never going to be. Every year, our grade school nurse measured our height and weight. I dreaded that day because she repeated the numbers aloud for her assistant to record. In fifth grade, when I got off the scale and the numbers were read, the petite curly-headed girl behind me in line said, "Geez, that's more than my mom weighs!" Too bad the nurse didn't provide self-esteem counseling. I was going to need that.

In my quest to be skinny, I started dieting at an early age. When you diet, you eat according to a plan, and it is always someone else's plan. No one would eat Melba toast and rice cakes voluntarily unless they were born with an insatiable desire to chew on Styrofoam.

Dieting requires choking down timbers of celery and other tasteless veggies like Bok Choy* because they

---

* As it turns out, Bok Choy was not a Communist dictator as I had previously thought, but rather, a tasteless vegetable designed to fill up your stomach like packing peanuts in a empty box. It's a miracle I matriculated at all.

are "free." In fact, celery supposedly burns "negative calories." If that were truly the case, I would have vanished into thin air by the time I was sixteen. After years of dieting, I was tired of counting pluses and minuses. Being on a diet is like being an accountant, but with food. You count points and carbs and even the number of times you chew each point and carb. You count pounds lost and gained as well as half pounds and quarter pounds lost and gained (but *never* the Quarter-pounders you ate in the parking lot when no one was watching you chew). You even count the pounds lost and gained by friends and coworkers who are dieting along with you. ("What am I going to eat today? What am I not going to eat today? What are you going to eat today? What are you not going to eat today?" Riveting conversation to a serious dieter.) In the end, the only number you care about counting is the number of days left until you can *stop* counting and eat whatever the heck you want.

Pregnancy was my chance to do just that, and I was perplexed by the freedom. The obstetrician's office wanted to weigh me every visit. They were delighted to see the scale inch up, a concept I could barely wrap my head around. I'd never been in a situation where weight gain was met with anything but disdain. I felt like a visitor in a strange new land.

As far back as I could remember, I only knew one truth and it was imprinted on my mind like cellulite on a thigh.

WEIGHT DOWN = GOOD

WEIGHT UP = BAD

With baby on board, that rule had changed. Now, up = good and down = bad. Seeing the scale climb every month caused anxiety, reminiscent of the disastrous diet club weigh-in where I'd used up three months worth of points with a single trip to the movie snack bar.

From an early age, I had a love/hate relationship with The Scale. We shared an on-again, off-again friendship, like the kind of fickle friendship offered by the popular girl at school. One day you're best friends, and the next day you're not speaking. When you're on good terms, all is well with the world. You are popular, beautiful, and the envy of all the other girls who would give anything to be in your position. If you fall out of favor, you become the subject of ridicule. You find yourself sitting alone in the cafeteria wondering what you could have done to earn their affection. You hate yourself for trying so hard to impress them, but you can't seem to help it. It's like *Mean Girls*, but with numbers.

I had weighed in at more than my share of diet clubs by this time. The weigh-in line at the scale resembles something of a strip club for overweight people. Shoes go first. It doesn't matter that shoes rarely weigh more than a pound or two; they are jettisoned like lead weights on a sinking ship. Dieters shed every last item of clothing allowable by law, as well as jewelry that is normally weighed in grams. All this, in the hopes of making the scale love you just a little bit more.

Stepping on a scale is an art form.* Expert dieters know how to step on the scale slowly and carefully, as if suddenly pouncing up on it would trick the scale into thinking you are heavier than you really are. Holding your breath is an important prerequisite. Sucking in your stomach makes it jump off into the next room where it doesn't count toward the overall total. Strict dieters know it's advantageous to step on the scale backwards, pausing for a moment to let the scale "settle" to an acceptable weight (preferably 110) while you're not looking.

When The Scale has finally settled, it's time to steal a *quick* glance at the numbers over the shoulder. The glance *has* to be quick.   This all-important

---

* Always consult your physician before starting any step-up plan on The Scale. Results may vary. Large weight loss not typical. Do not expect a huge loss in a short amount of time even if these miraculous results are advertised on TV, magazines, radio, and billboards. Read the fine print. Easy weight loss is never what it appears, and if it sounds too good to be true, somebody is making a ton of money off of it.

quick-glance-method gives your brain time to tally the numbers and send the results directly to your subconscious. Once the subconscious acknowledges the outcome, it is double-checked for accuracy and plugged into a pre-existing formula which was designed by your Internal Affairs Department years before. The final outcome is officially announced to your fragile ego, affecting not only your overall feelings of self-worth, but how you will treat yourself (and others) for the rest of the day.

Even if weight loss *has* occurred, any amount less than hoped for has the potential to cause devastation. (What? Seven days of cottage cheese and kale rolls, and all I lost is twenty pounds? Forget this crap!) It is of little consolation to remind the disappointed dieter that any weight lost, even a small amount, is a positive step toward their overall health goals. You have to remember that "Scale fail" is like beauty; it is in the eyes of the beholder. Unfortunately, any perceived failure has the potential to trigger a swift and counterproductive visit to Dairy Queen, sometimes accompanied by other less-than-thrilled Waist Watchers. Medicating your mind with an entire box of Dilly Bars feels great at the moment, but it also wipes out all your available points until Christmas.

The best-case scenario is a pleasant numerical reading, registering a loss that is well within the hoped-for range. Such a reading can release more endorphins than a dump truck full of Prozac. "Good" numbers register quickly with the Internal Affairs department, initiating a psychological shower of balloons and confetti. Your internal cheerleading squad applauds you by shouting "Congratulations! You did it!" with all the fanfare of a Publishers Clearing House commercial. You feel relief and love and a sense of self-worth, like that sweet moment you opened the invitation to the popular girl's sleepover party when you thought you'd been left off the list.

When the HG finally subsided, I gained the required amount of weight and began to "show," although most of my prenatal girth remained in my upper body. As my belly grew, so did people's curiosity with it. Everywhere I went, people touched my baby bump as though their hand was drawn to it like a magnet. Some folks went for the tender pat-pat-pat, while others rubbed it with gentle gusto, like it was Lincoln's nose at the Springfield, Illinois monument.*

Some women don't care for the belly rubs, but I embraced them wholeheartedly. After what I'd been through, they felt like high fives as I rounded the last third of the maternal marathon. A cup of water would have been nice too, but who's whining.

Something magical happened during this spontan-

---

* Like every kid who grew up in Illinois, I went on a mandatory field trip to the Capital. There was a clearly posted sign by the copper statue of Lincoln's head which said DO NOT TOUCH. Everyone did it anyhow. Why can't people follow rules? I could. I wanted to see someone arrested for it, but that would never happen. All the Illinois police are at O'Hare Airport ready to pounce on little Smart Alecs who make innocent jokes about exploding suitcases.

eous Baby-meld.*   People began to tell me their own stories of how they "started their families" (a phrase I heard myself saying, though I swore I never would). Some of the most heartfelt stories were birthed entirely outside of a delivery room.   While my HG had been a challenge, it seemed like a small sacrifice compared to the months and sometimes years couples wait in order to welcome a child into their lives. Foster parenting, adoption, and marriage into a ready-made family are just some of the creative ways in which God grows a family tree. (In some states, the family tree looks more like a wreath; but that's a topic for another day.)

As I listened, I felt a flush of excitement about joining this Sorority called Motherhood. I just wasn't sure I would fit in. I desperately hoped my sorority sisters would not be disappointed in their newest pledge.

---

* A Spock reference my fellow Trekkies would recognize. I am a science geek at heart. Live long and prosper my friends.

Chapter 15

Waiting for the ~~Bloody~~ Show
to Start

"For the love of God folks, don't try this at home."
David Letterman

Even though our decision to have children was nonchalant, one thing Fred and I were both adamant about was keeping the sex of our baby a surprise until birth. It felt too much like sneaking a peek at Christmas presents before the big day.

Given our genetic combination, we already knew Uncle Ben wasn't going to be Greek, Royal, or long-legged. As cliché as it sounds, all we wanted was a healthy baby. However, I wouldn't have complained if I gave birth to a thick-haired supermodel that married a member of the Greek Royal family, who just happened to have a yacht on central time. That would have at least given me the opportunity to live my life out vicariously through my child, something parents are famous for.

Secretly, I wished for a boy because I wasn't sure I would know what to do with a daughter. I didn't really know what to do with a son either, but I was pretty certain I could teach him how to get out the door in ten minute or less. I never said I wanted a son out loud, for the same reason I never publicly verbalized my secret desire to be a supermodel. At least I had a 50% chance of having a boy. I had less than a 5% chance of being a supermodel. Disappointment is always a possibility. A public announcement virtually guarantees it.

As the due date neared, folks constantly asked two questions: what was the sex of the baby, and what we were going to name whatever it was we had. Fred and I didn't mean to, but we frustrated those folks by keeping mum on both topics.

First of all, we didn't *know* the sex of the child, so we honestly had no answer for them. This statement was routinely met with wide eyes and a gasp of disbelief. "You don't *want* to *know*? Why not? Why don't you *want* to *know*? Are you afraid of technology? Are you Amish? Even Amish people would w*ant* to *know*, if they could. (But they can't.) Everybody finds out these days!"

This emotional shockwave was immediately followed by an equally amusing battery of insipid questions. "Don't you *need* to *know*? Don't you *want* to *plan*? Don't you *know* that you *need* to *plan*? How can you *plan* if you don't want to *know*?" It was like talking to Dr. Seuss. I had already planned on not sleeping for the next decade. What else was there to plan for, exactly?

Since the beginning of time, people have had babies without knowing what kind of plumbing they were equipped with, and everything worked out just fine. People acted like our baby would end up naked on the street because we didn't know whether to buy a pink or blue Onesie months ahead of time. Newborn's have fuzzy vision at first, so they could care less if the nursery was decorated with blue bears or pink princesses the minute they got home from the hospital. Parents are the ones who care, not the babies.

Secondly, even if we *did* know the sex of the baby, Fred and I weren't sharing our names with anyone - friend or foe. It was too risky. We didn't want to tell anyone because, quite frankly, we didn't want to hear their reaction to our choice of names. A single "innocent" comment can a destroy a previously loved name like a mental wrecking ball.

That may sound harsh, but be honest. Have you ever known folks to hold their tongue when they *don't* like a baby name? Comments such as "Amanda? That's a nice name. Very pretty. That reminds me of a girl I went to grade school with. Her name was Amanda. Strange girl. Her nose was the size of a cucumber. Come to think of it, she wet her pants every day in gym class too." Okay, so forget Amanda.

Or how about "Benjamin? Good choice. Benjamin's a strong name. A good, Biblical name. Have you ever seen that movie Benjamin Button? Good movie. Strange ending though. When Benjamin was old, he looked like a shrunken little man with the face of a dehydrated apple." Thanks folks. Now we hate *that* name too, and we are not very fond of you anymore either.

So, in an effort to protect our friendships, we decided some things are just better kept to ourselves.

I wished I hadn't left so much to do toward the end of the pregnancy, but I couldn't help it. Had I shopped during those first two trimesters, I would have left a permanent stain (not to mention odor) on all my purchases. With less than a month to go, I still needed a car seat, a high chair, and a stroller. If I didn't get a move on, I'd be walking home with the baby, and I was pretty sure that wouldn't be safe, comfortable, or entirely legal.

Much to my dismay (and discomfort), ninth-month errands were not executed with the same dexterity and speed as sixth-month errands. Walking had become waddling. Standing was heavy lifting, even when my arms were empty. The most mundane task was more challenging now that my center of gravity had shifted to the next zip code. My baby bump was even bumping into objects I couldn't see in my direct line of vision, a contradiction to every law I had learned in physics.

I thought about designing a hat with a large angled mirror perched on it, like they have in the grocery store. That way I could at least shout "Fore!" right before my protruding belly smacked into oncoming traffic. It was a good idea, but alas, that entrepreneurial venture would have to wait until I launched my chain of childfree restaurants, *and* my line of clothing for fashion-backward engineers.

At this point, I had gained a little over 20 pounds. Half of it must have been in the form of an internal bowling ball, because something down there was rolling back and forth across my bladder every time I moved. Suddenly, laughter was nothing to sneeze at, and sneezing was nothing to laugh at. Once again, incontinence was my constant companion. I felt like one of the *Golden Girls* way before my time (which wouldn't have been so bad had I actually gotten to work with my hero, Betty White).

On a daily basis, I experienced shooting pains in the nether region, as though Uncle Ben was knocking on the door to freedom but couldn't get anyone to pay attention. Every time I stood up, I waved a hand between my thighs, feeling for the dangling leg or protruding umbilical cord that felt like it had fallen out. My doctor reassured me that all of these discomforts were "normal." Sure. I'd like to see *her* squeeze in and out of a tiny VW Rabbit when *she's* the size of Shamu. It was anything but "normal."

Another "normal" sensation came in the form of Braxton-Hicks contractions, or false labor. These are the body's equivalent of a uterine dress rehearsal. Apparently, wombs require practice to be sure they know what to do when the big moment arrives. I was a little disappointed in my uterus' performance during these rehearsals. My practice contractions were laughable at best. (Didn't they know that practice made perfect?) They felt more like a half-hearted sit-up than an important birthing run-through. I sincerely hoped my uterus would step it up a notch. My mammary glands were definitely taking this whole thing seriously, so I hoped my womb would straighten up and follow suit. Perhaps some internal organs are just more dedicated than others.

I waited with great anticipation for the "mucus plug" to plop out, but mostly out of curiosity. Some medical terms should be changed so as not to offend the general public. That was one of them. (I was grossed out and I was a nurse for crying out loud.)

Having never seen a mucus plug, I wondered what the experience would entail. Would it sound like a rubber stopper being plucked from a bathtub, followed by a sudden gush of sudsy water and a sparkling clean newborn? I could only pray it would be that easy.

In addition to the mucus plug, there was the "bloody show" to look forward to. Again, I had no idea what to expect. (Another great candidate for new terminology. *Please*.) By all accounts, a show should be entertaining, with terrific actors, buttered popcorn, and thunderous applause. This wasn't going to be even close.

I was afraid to walk around in public because the bottom might fall out - literally. Without warning, my amniotic dam could collapse, causing a flood of who-knows-what to spill out on to the floor, like a bloody water-main break. No one in their right mind would buy a ticket to *that* show (myself included). I didn't know if other pregnant women carried around a splat mat and squeegee, but I thought it sounded like a good idea so I kept one in the car "just in case." One thing was certain; I was not going to be caught dead sitting on anyone's sofa until this whole thing was over. Especially if it was white.

A month or so from our due date, Fred and I were invited to a friend's home for lunch and babysitting; at least, that's what they called it. By the end, it felt more like a baby intervention than a social call, like our friends were trying to tell us: "YOU ARE NOT READY FOR THIS AND EVERYONE KNOWS IT!" They wanted to give us a little real-time experience by spending time with their kid. It's as though they were worried parents, and we were hapless teenagers applying for a driver's license without enough practice hours.*

---

* *Fifty hours of driving practice are required to apply for a license in the state of Ohio. Ironically, it is not necessary to practice a single hour for parenthood. And we think driving causes a lot of wreckage?*

During the inter-visit-vention, the couple's six-month-old cried quite a bit. Mom described him as a "happy baby." If that was the case, I'd hate to see her version of an unhappy baby. I never saw babies cry non-stop on soap operas or *Little House on the Prairie*, although I once read that TV babies were usually twins who were traded out when they became fussy. Just another reason you can't believe everything you see on television.

Not only was I flabbergasted that in real life "happy babies" had crying jags, I was also dismayed to learn that infants have their own sense of time. Apparently, baby minutes are to regular minutes what dog years are to human years, basically a 7:1 ratio. Crybaby's Mother said he often played with his toys for a "long time," which she went on to define as 10-15 minutes. In her mind, that was a long time. In my mind, that was less time than it took to get off the phone with a telemarketer. What had I gotten myself into?

What if I inherited a sad baby, or one that couldn't entertain itself for longer than a nano-second? What if her little whine-bag wasn't a fluke? What if there were more like him? More importantly, what if they were headed straight for me? My mind started to race.

What if Fred and I didn't have a perfect smiling baby like the one on the applesauce jar? Why didn't I think of this before? I was mad at myself for being so easily duped by the Gerber marketing people. (My grandmother called it being flimflammed. I called it being gullible.) What if we had a constant crier, like a baby with colic? Colicky babies can cry for hours, days, sometimes even weeks on end. What then? Was there a return policy? How about a warranty? I never made any major purchase without a warranty.

I started to panic.

I knew there were parents who had to deal with difficult children, but I never thought it could happen to me. This was the first time it dawned on me that no one asked for volunteers when it came to doling out fussy children, or any other high need child for that matter. God did not bestow the difficult ones only upon those who were saintly long-suffering types with the patience of Job. He did not ask for a resume that proved you could hack it, or a show of hands indicating that you wanted to give it the ol' college try.

No one was guaranteed a compliant child because they had checked all the boxes, went to Sunday school every week, or knew the 23rd Psalm by heart. You could be the Pope and it wouldn't matter. (Ok, so that's not a good example, but you know what I mean.) Parenthood was more like a baby lottery, and I had already bought a ticket. It is the only lottery in existence where you get a guaranteed lifetime payout just for playing. I just prayed that I wouldn't win the Powerball Puker, the Super Screamer, or the Wildcard Whiner.

In light of all these emotions, I began to see women without children in an entirely different light. Childless females are often unfairly stereotyped as uncaring, just because they don't have children. True, some women are career focused and would rather break glass ceilings than clean messy fingerprints off of them. (Who can blame them? On the other hand, maybe they've never tried cleaning with a tiara on. That changes everything. At least it did for me.) The bottom line is some women simply don't want children, and that's perfectly alright.

For the first time, however, I had empathy for a group of women I had never paid attention to before; those who decide to forgo having children not because they don't want them, but for reasons most of us will never know or understand. These women are not selfish, they are self-aware, opting out of motherhood altogether in order to protect the best interest of their would-be child. Not every woman is cut out to be a mother, and it takes courage to acknowledge that. It takes even more courage to say it out loud.

I began to wonder if I was one of those women and should have recognized it long before

I brought Uncle Ben into the picture. I'd always heard the saying, "God won't give you more than you can handle." I desperately hoped He and I saw eye-to-eye on just how much that was.

Chapter 16

The Times Have ~~Barely~~ Changed

"Childbirth is like taking your bottom lip
and pulling it over your head."
Carol Burnett

Two weeks before my due date I got up
in the middle of the night to make a sandwich. It
took me a full twenty minutes just to visualize
the sequence of aerobic events that would need
to take place before I could hoist my gargantuan girth
off the mattress.

Once the snack was down the hatch,
I waddled back down hall toward the bedroom.
I felt something warm trickle down my leg. "Gosh
darn it," I thought. "I am peeing on myself again."
But this time it was different. The sensation increased
with each step, leaving a trail behind me on the carpet
like an old car leaking oil.

Where was the mucus plug? Did I miss the bloody show? Hopefully, I had not left any organic matter laying on the kitchen floor where Fred would step in it, or the dogs could have at it. Either way, my water bag had definitely broken. It was time to take action.

I stared at Fred as he lay drooling on his pillow. I could hear him make that little slurping sound night-droolers make when they unconsciously retract the spit that's forming a stream across their pillow. Thankfully he hadn't hit heavy flow mode yet, or I would have needed a paddle to get to him.

I paused for a moment and gazed at Fred's lightly freckled, pale Irish skin in the glow of the hallway light, feeling both giddy and guilty about waking my sweet young husband with the news that fatherhood was about to change his life forever. I wasn't exactly sure how to do it.

Waking a man from a dead sleep is never easy, unless of course, the promise of food is involved. (Even then, it's a crapshoot.) Plus, Fred had a tendency to overreact to all things medical (nosebleeds, hangnails, that sort of thing). I had to be careful in my approach, especially in the middle of the night. A blaring pronouncement of impending labor might induce panic, and that wouldn't be pretty. On the other hand, giving him a matter-of-fact, medically-oriented update would have confused poor, sleepy Fred. He might have thought he was having a nightmare.

I contemplated going with a macho-man-MacGyver-type approach, using the illustration "Yippee Kai-yay Fred! You know that baby bomb that's been ticking for the last eight months? Well, apparently the red wire thingy, and the blue wire thingy just crossed. It's going to detonate any moment and make you a Daddy! Let's get to the hospital for the big explosion!" Looking back, that's what I should have said. That would have made sense to Fred.

Instead, I took the Hollywood approach. Having clearly watched *way* too much sappy television (when will I learn?), I leaned into Fred's ear and uttered the grand cliché all movie women use to announce they are going into labor:

"Honey…I think it's time."

I stepped back, waiting for the characteristically chaotic television antics to unfold. Any moment now, Fred was going to turn into the stereotypical father-to-be who frantically jumps in the car and speeds toward the hospital, leaving his expectant wife in the driveway holding a suitcase. The abandoned wife just stands in the driveway, grinning patiently while her adorably daft baby daddy backs up and retrieves her before making a mad dash to the delivery room. Why any woman would just stand there and not wave down her dippy husband before he was fully out of the driveway was beyond me. Why she was smiling about it, I'll never understand. Sometimes common sense ruins perfectly good television.

It should not come as a shock to anyone at this point that the TV scenario was not the one that unfolded at our house. Instead of the traditional pop-your-head-off-the-pillow reaction I had expected, Fred yawned drowsily and queried, "How much longer can I sleep?" That was it. No antics. No rushing. No nothing. I was getting ready to have a baby, and I'd seen my husband more panicked over an ingrown toenail.

I stared in disbelief as a steady stream of amniotic fluid christened our brand new carpet. This situation was a little more pressing than your average nosebleed, yet Fred was as cool as a cucumber. My darling engineer methodically remind-ed me that we didn't actually *need* to go to the hospital until my contractions were five minutes apart. Since I wasn't having any contractions yet, he thought it was the perfect time to get a little extra shuteye.

In response to my dumbfounded expression, Fred was determined to prove his point. He began calculating the drop-dead time of departure using the Pythagorean theorem, the table of elements, and the absence of contractions as variables. After quoting his projections like Socrates on steroids, I advised him that he should start making new calculations based on how long it would be before I strangled him with the growing stack of towels between my thighs. Doing the "new math," he suddenly decided we should get moving sooner rather than later. (Good choice, Freddy Boy.)

Someday I am going to write a television script about the lives of women married to engineers and call it "The Daze of our Wives." For marketing and promotional purposes, it will be released at the same time as my companion clothing line, Garengineers.

Rubbing his eyes, Fred groggily informed me that we were out of camera batteries, and he hopped in the car to hunt for more. I was sure that my contractions would kick in momentarily, so while Fred was on his battery run, I jumped in the shower for a quick scrub down.

I smoothed and shaved everything I could reach, which wasn't much at this point. I never could reach my heels, which was a real bummer because they'd started to cling to the carpet like Velcro.

As an employee of the hospital, I didn't want the nurses in Labor & Delivery to see me this way, lest they think I'd "let myself go" prematurely. It would have been embarrassing to plop my feet up in stirrups with a thicket of hair around my ankles, after prancing into the delivery room like a Clydesdale. I was tempted to braid my leg locks and put little beads on the end, telling people I'd recently been to

Cancun. Instead, I decided to wait until Fred got home to help me dethatch.

As I stood in the shower, reality hit me in the face as hard and fast as the water drops. This baby is going to come out of my body today. It will be extracted in one of two ways...*and neither option is remotely appealing.* I had always laughed about Carol Burnett's description of childbirth with her clever "pull your lip over your head" routine, but somehow it's not nearly as hilarious when you're the one reaching for your lip.

I waited for Fred to return and my labor to begin, neither of which was happening any time soon. I told my uterus this wasn't a dress rehearsal but it seemed to be tuning me out altogether. Since Fred was taking forever, I had time to think about silly things, like what it would have been like to have the first baby ever, and about my mom's account of giving birth on a military base. Between Eve, my mother's generation, and myself, the whole process had come full circle, as so many things in life do.

Maternity wear was a perfect example. Eve walked around the Garden of Eden wearing nothing but fig leaves, while my mother's generation hid their growing bellies under tent-tops like they were trying to hide their pregnancy from the world. Reverting back to the more natural look, today's moms proudly flaunt their baby bumps by wearing nothing but string bikinis at the pool. Like I said, we've come full circle. (Well, almost.)

As far as the actual delivery, I suspect Eve had her baby the only way she knew how, by screaming at the top of her lungs until she saw something plop out into the dirt. One might assume Adam performed the role of catcher, but without knowing what he was supposed to be catching, he might easily have missed. Watching that historical interaction play out for the first time would have made the best reality TV finale ever. It's funny enough to watch a man hold a baby for the first time, even when he knows what an infant looks like. I can't imagine how hysterical it would have been to watch Adam, particularly the part where he had to cut the cord with no instruction manual. I would have paid real money to see that.

My mother's generation gave birth in a sterilized operating room, with the aid of heavy sedation and a professional obstetrician (as opposed to a clueless male prototype with a missing rib). Only the medical staff was allowed to be in the room. Fathers were relegated to an overcrowded waiting room where they paced for hours. Their only job was to wring their hands with worry. When the doctor finally appeared, and the all's-well-with-mother-and-child thumbs up was given, the new dad's biggest role was to look relieved while passing out celebratory, albeit cancer-causing, cigars.

In those days, a stern-looking nurse in a starched white hat whisked the newborn away to a nursery where he or she would join other new squealing arrivals. There, they would be fed a bottle of modern, new-fangled formula, rather than wait for the old-fashioned mammary milk truck to show up.

After Eve delivered, she probably bathed herself, and the baby, in a nearby stream, latched the suckling newborn onto her breast, and went back to picking fruit or whatever it was she was doing when the first pangs of labor signaled something big was up down below. No doubt by that time she had more than her postnatal share of regrets about biting into that Garden-fresh apple. The indescribable pain of childbirth might have been offset somewhat had she traded it for a caramel apple with nuts, and chocolate and stuff on it. But all that misery for a plain, organic apple? What *was* she thinking.

Yes, childbirth had come full circle. Hospitals across the land now focused on giving patients a "natural" birthing experience. Fred and I jumped on that bandwagon by taking classes designed to help us manage the pain of childbirth without the use of drugs.

A Registered Nurse Midwife taught us the Lamaze technique, a child-extraction plan promoting pain-free, drug-free (and by all accounts, fun-free) births. With the Lamaze technique, pain control is accomplished by hoo-hooing and hee-heeing your way to parenthood while focusing on anything but the searing pain ripping through your hoo-ha.

Fred and I attended classes religiously and listened intently as our instructor (whom I affectionately referred to as Mother Earth) espoused natural childbirth as the superior path to a harmonious life entry. We practiced faithfully, determined to make Uncle Ben's transition from womb to world as "natural" as possible.

A lot more than pain control had changed since my mother's birthing days. Delivery rooms had been redesigned in an effort to be more "earthy" and less sanitized, kind of like Starbucks, but with nurses. There were soft lights overhead, wooden floors below, and mood music in surround. Some facilities even offered romantic twilight dinners to the exhausted but happy parents only minutes after the baby is born. (Petite filet anyone? Right after the placenta falls out? Thanks, but I think I'll pass.)

Women no longer took contractions lying down, as previous generations had. Heck no. Modern laborers were encouraged to walk in circles, do jumping jacks or perform cartwheels until fully dilated. If labor failed to progress, there was always the half-marathon option, where pregnant women waddle swiftly around the halls of the maternity ward with all the intensity of an impromptu track and field event.

The father's role had changed as well. In fact, his job description had undergone the biggest overhaul of all. Dads were not only *allowed* at the mother's bedside, now they were expected to *coach* the whole ordeal from the sidelines like an experienced Olympic trainer. Duties included therapeutic massage, psychological counseling, and dee-jaying with a mash-up of mom's favorite tunes. Dad was also Head Cheerleader for each and every contraction, often forming the base of a pyramid for other cheerleaders who came to join the birthing party.

Strict visiting hours were a thing of the past. Practically any Tom, Dick or Harry* could join the hospital birthday bash. Siblings, friends, and even vaguely familiar neighbors were permitted in the delivery room at any hour of the day or night. Even complete strangers could squeeze in and sing "Kum Ba Yah" while holding hands, as long as those hands were disinfected with antimicrobial gel.

Once the baby was successfully extracted, co-workers, pen pals, or even your favorite UPS delivery guy could cut the umbilical cord with pinking shears, as long as they were sterile (the shears, not the UPS guy).

Poor Eve had only her memory to recount the events of her child's birth. Sure, she could ask Adam, but if he was like most men, he forgot a few minor details such as the name, weight, and sex of the baby. Thanks to modern technology, it was now possible to videotape the whole event in living color to share at the next family reunion or office Christmas party. Some folks may find it "natural" to have an audience stare at your lady parts during delivery, but Fred and I preferred to keep our private footage private.

---

* *I've never met these men personally, but my mother referred to them constantly; so I assumed they would show up eventually.*

If couples were really trendy, a water birth was the way to go. This allowed the infant to ease from one aquatic venue to another without a harsh disturbance in The Force. I knew a wonderful mother who had all of her babies this way, in the bathtub at home. She said the last few kiddos came so fast she never even had time to summon the midwife. By baby number twelve, she was a pro, sliding the baby into the bathwater with only a gentle contraction or two.

After summoning her extended family to view the newest member, Mom handed off the baby to her eldest daughter, a twenty something, presumably working on a nearby loom. She then proceeded to finish shaving her legs before yanking out the placenta, which was used to plant a commemorative tree with every birth. Their yard probably resembles a National Forest by now.

Regardless of birth method, it was now hip to place the still-slimy infant immediately upon the mother's chest in order to jumpstart the all-important bonding process. Good mommies, the ones who were born with maternal know-how oozing from every pore, could intuitively latch the suckling child onto her breast in one fell swoop, offering a lifetime of antibodies and self-esteem in a few precious gulps.

Some women's anatomy made for an easy latch-on. Those are probably the same gals who can comfortably get away without wearing a bra. I'd heard that only women who can not hold a pencil under their breasts should go braless. I could hold a small printer under mine; suffice it to say, breastfeeding wasn't going to be easy. I might need a third hand and a forklift to facilitate feedings.

If the infant nursed with ease, the mother-child bond was in the bag, prompting choruses of oohs and aahs from onlookers, like a crowd watching Fourth of July fireworks. However, if breastfeeding was a complete bust, you were automatically enrolled in the BFD (Breastfeeding For Dummies). This class was for remedial feeders, and was taught by a buddy of Mother's Earth's who was the Lactation Champion in the state of California for 20 years in a row.

In other words, this was not your mother's delivery. Times had definitely changed.

My wandering thoughts were disrupted by Fred as he bellowed my name and dumped a year's supply of batteries and snacks on the bed. It looked as though we were going camping for a month instead of to the hospital for a couple of days. The reality of the situation must have caught up to Fred's brain, because he insisted we leave before my hair was camera-ready, something he would never have done under normal circumstances.

As I waddled to the car, Fred read the checklist aloud:

- *Hospital bag, which included a brand new pink night gown that made me look like a giant frosted cupcake. Check.*

- *Rolling pin, focal point, and Lamaze handbook with step by step instructions on how to drop the baby out in Grapes-of-Wrath fashion as we had practiced. Check.*

- *Birthing music written by Mozart designed to trick our baby into thinking he was the next Einstein. Check.*

- *Video recorder the size of a bazooka with a lifetime supply of batteries. Check.*

- *Squeaky clean, half-coifed wife who was scared to death about what kind of mother she would be.*

Check, check, and double check.

Chapter 17

Failure to ~~See Life as a Work in~~ Progress

"If pregnancy were a book, they would cut out
the last two chapters."
Nora Ephron

I was expecting a festive welcome at the hospital, like the kind you see on TV when a pregnant woman bursts into the emergency room declaring she is in labor. I assumed I would be surrounded by a herd of excited nurses falling all over themselves to greet me with people-pleasing glee. I was sure there would be rushing, important medical chatter, and an enthusiastic frenzy of anticipation for the impending miracle of life. I got a clipboard and a wristband. It was a rather disappointing reception to say the least.

Perhaps my lack of gut-wrenching groans and mind-blowing contractions kept me from getting the top shelf service I thought I deserved. Apparently, women who roll through the doors with a full head of ringlets protruding between their legs are taken more seriously. Whatever.

Had I known *that,* I would have laced my arrival with a blood-curdling scream, shouting "I'm crowning! With twins!" I don't usually lie, but hey, all I wanted was a whirlwind ride to the maternity ward in a wheelchair, like Wilma Flintstone got. To be honest, I felt a little ripped off.

An hour later, I had filled out enough paperwork to kill five trees, and still no contractions. Nada. Zip. Zero. I tried talking nicely to my belly, and massaging it gently in hopes of getting a reaction. My uterus remained mum. It continued to be the same stubborn, unimpressive mechanical dud it had been during rehearsals. I decided to give *it* the silent treatment.

When that didn't work, it was time to force the issue. I was going to show my body just *who was boss.* I closed my eyes and bore down hard, producing a hearty grunt for emphasis. Nothing. I felt like a rabid fan at a baseball game desperately trying to get "the wave" started in a section filled with cranky old golfers. It just wasn't happening.

I discovered an interesting fact during that futile exercise. While it may be possible to control almost every muscle in your body, there are two muscles you definitely can NOT control at will: your heart, and your uterus. You can hold your breath until you pass out. You can burp the alphabet on command. You can cross your eyes and hold your pee until your tongue floats, but you cannot cross your heart and hope to die, or force a contraction no matter how hard you try. It simply can't be done.

This was beyond frustrating to me. I hated having no control. It was as maddening as being at a complete standstill on the highway. I would rather drive ten miles out of my way just so I could be moving. Mentally, I honked at my female parts with all the verve of a New York taxi driver. It did as much good as laying on the horn in the middle of a city traffic jam (although us Chicagoans love to do it anyway).*

Another two hours went by and still nothing. The labor and delivery staff was as frustrated as I was. Either that, or they were bored from hours of watching me belch and honk the sides of my belly with my thumbs. So, they decided to call in a nurse they called The Big Guns. I was ready to go back home, that is, until I met her. Nurse BG was a Jamaican-born

---

* Airbags have taken all the joy out of "colorfully educating others on how to drive." I can't tell you how many times I've honked my air bag at a passer-by who deserved a good honking-to, but didn't get it because the stupid airbags are now where the horn used to be. I'm sorry, but pushing the little trumpet symbol on either side of the steering wheel with your thumbs does not have the same endorphin release as a straight-up-palm-in-the-middle-press-like-you-mean-it blast. I have never gotten in trouble for my "driver's education communication," but probably because the horn has been moved from the middle. I guess I do have air bags to thank for saving my life after all.

midwife with beautiful brown skin and a dazzling white smile.

I wondered if they referred to her as The Big Guns because she was the best midwife in her class, or because she had some sort of scary Jamaican voodoo that coerced an infant out of the womb. Typically I would vote for the former, but at this point, voodoo sounded better than sitting still waiting for something to happen so I didn't balk. I just wanted to get the baby out so I could finish doing the back of my hair before Fred started rolling the video camera.

Voodoo or not, I really liked her. There was something inherently reassuring about this woman. She oozed maternal experience, as well as medical know-how. Plus, every word she uttered was laced with that soothing Caribbean accent, which kind of made me feel like I was on vacation. Her presence was both authoritative and calming, like an enigmatic mix of Bob Marley and Florence Nightingale (aka "Flo-Bob"). "No prah-blom Mee-suz Bow-kee. We go-na get dees bay-bee oat soon." All that was missing was a steel drum band and a fruity drink with a little umbrella in it.

Awhile later, it was clear to the Jamaican Wonder that my private parts weren't doing their job, so she ordered a jump-starting drug called Pitocin to be dump-ed into my IV. Even though it was a relief to finally get things rolling, I was overwhelmed with defeat. I watched our highly anticipated dream of a "natural" birth ebb away drop by drop. I began to cry.

It wasn't long before I felt the powerful pharmaceutical bully coerce my cervix into dilating. Natural contractions start slowly and gradually build in intensity. Not Pitocin contractions. They come at you hard and fast, creating a wham-pow-have-a-baby-now sensation that is hard to describe, and even harder to tolerate.

Pitocin contractions feel like a pit bull has clamped down on your uterus, holding it there until it decides to drop it like a rag doll. You can hardly catch your breath before the dog comes back and clamps down again, this time with even more force than before.*

Instead of breathing and panting in rhythmic fashion like I was supposed to, I held my breath and cursed at the Lamaze Chick in my mind. The pain was so intense, I feared I would implode from the inside out. Given my pained expression, my sweaty hair, and red, blotchy face, it was safe to say there weren't going to be any shining moments captured on film here for posterity. What a shame. Filling our empty mantel with framed Kodak moments was one of the reasons we were having a baby in the first place.

---

* Fred has since questioned my example because I've never actually been bitten in the uterus by a pit bull. (Oh really? Says who.) That wasn't the point. I doubt most people have actually been "stuck with a hot poker," or "hit in the head with a baseball bat" either, but you hear those phrases to describe bodily pain all the time and nobody gives them any grief.

After hours of serial killer contractions, I was exhausted. Florence Marley came in to check my progress, and I anticipated a glowing report after all this excruciating effort. She called it a "quick check." I called it scratching my nose from the inside, with a glancing blow to my liver and spleen along the way.

After retrieving the entire length of her arm from my innards, she snapped off her glove and somberly announced that I was dilated to a whopping one centimeter. "WHAT? ONE CENTIMETER? ARE YOU KIDDING ME? AFTER ALL THAT?" I fully expected to hear that I was at least eight, maybe nine centimeters dilated. Even then I would have been disappointed. But ONE? One was nothing. I'll bet Flo-Bob was dilated to one and she was just standing there.

About that time, Fred started to ~~whine,~~ er, ~~complain,~~ er, I mean communicate, that he was hungry. "Whaaaat did you just say Fred?" I asked rhetorically. Did he not hear what the glove-snapping-gizzard-squeezing-Rasta-nurse just said? I'd been working like a fiend for hours with nothing to show for it, and all he could think about was FOOD? Of all the nerve.

How did he think I felt? Did he think this was some sort of beach vacation for me, and the gurney was a blow up raft? This was no picnic for me either. I was hungry *and* in pain, but you didn't hear *me* whining about it. (By the way, pain trumps hunger. The combination of both trumps everything, especially during labor.) I would have given a thousand dollars for a cheeseburger right then, but I was NPO (Nothing By Mouth in medical terms, Notably Put Out in mine).

I was incensed when he loudly inquired as to where the cafeteria was. I'd never seen any television husband do that in all my life. Perhaps I missed the *one* episode called *Tending to Your Husband's Low Blood Sugar While Extruding His Heir*, but I seriously doubt it. I'd seen a lot of television.

I watched in disbelief as the nurse politely gave Fred directions to the cafeteria, as though his needs were equal to mine. It was as unthinkable as catering to the Maid of Honor instead of the Bride on her wedding day. I thought I knew what to expect when I was expecting, but nobody told me to expect *that*.

I was tired, crabby and miserable, but not just physically. Mentally, I was worn out. Why was it so hard for me to do what zillions of women seemed to sail through effortlessly? (Comparing yourself to other women in the midst of gut-wrenching labor is a terrible idea if ever there was one.)

Of course Fred needed a break. He was only human. We had both been sweating for hours, like Richard Simmons* dancing to the oldies. It was a good thing Fred got to eat when he did because in the next

---

* *Google Mr. Simmons. It's worth a good chuckle...or two.*

few moments I was going to need him to be something I never wanted to ask of anyone. I needed him to be strong enough for the *both* of us.

After twenty hours of unproductive labor, Flo-Bob informed us that a C-section was inevitable. She knew we would be disappointed, and she was right. "Ahm so sah-dee Mee-suz Bow-kee. I know yoo hab tride sooo hah-d." The Big-hearted Guns gently explained that the problem was with my birth canal. It was very small, and too narrow for the baby's head to pass through. Who'da thunk it. I didn't know that us "big-boned gals" could even have a tiny pelvis.

I overheard Jamaica tell the staff to prepare a surgical suite, reciting the diagnosis of Failure to Progress. I wish she hadn't called it that. Even though I knew it was the technically appropriate term, "failure" was all I heard. My heart sank.

Why couldn't I have a "normal" birth? Didn't God know how hard I had tried? Wasn't He watching? After all, "natural childbirth" was His idea in the first place, wasn't it? Then why didn't He make it an equal opportunity venture? I thought I should have been rewarded for checking all the right boxes, and following all the rules. Fred and I went to class, practiced, and kept our snarky comments about Mother Earth to ourselves. Despite all that, a C-section was how it had to go down? Really?

After all I had been through with morning

sickness, I thought it only fair that God would throw me a bone when it came time to deliver. Hadn't I already done my time? The least He could do was let the kid slip out with little more than a hiccup. Apparently, He was not on board with my plan. This led me to wonder, was this how motherhood would always be for me, a constant struggle to get it right?

I was pretty sure Ma Ingalls never "failed" to progress. She could probably dilate her cervix simply by thinking about it. On the other hand, perhaps all those petticoats were just a clever disguise for Ma's embarrassingly giant pelvis. (One could only hope. It's not too late to start a few rumors.)

Yes, there was a silver lining in this whole frustrating ordeal. If nothing else, I was going to walk away with the small, but giddy pleasure of knowing that I was truly petite after all. Even if it *was* in places *not* visible to the naked eye.

Chapter 18

The Birth of a
~~Scared Out of Her Wits~~ Mother

*"One word frees us of all the weight and pain
in life. That word is love."*
Sophocles

The C-section wasn't nearly as "natural" as I had hoped. There were bright lights, suction machines, and an array of surgical tools on a tray next to me. It was kind of like being at the dentist for a root canal, except that they were working on the wrong end, and I was not going to get a free toothbrush when I left.

The nurse placed a cloth drape over my neck to prevent me from seeing what was going on below the waist, a completely unnecessary step. Had they seen my ankles *before* Fred used a machete on them, they would have known that I hadn't been able to see south of Baby Everest for weeks, and wouldn't have bothered with the drape.

The anesthesiologist placed a two-pronged oxygen tube in my nose that itched the whole time like a fuzzy caterpillar crawling back and forth across my upper lip.

My arms were outstretched to either side, and my legs were secured to the table, or so I was told. The epidural was in full effect, so I could have been doing a little jig for all I knew. Too bad my thighs didn't feel that weightless on a regular basis.

Fred was ushered to my side by the same bleeding-heart nurse who gave him directions to the cafeteria. He was gowned, gloved, and masked in anticipation of the Big Reveal.

Like most men, poor Fred had absolutely no idea what was coming next. Childbirth is a view to beat all views. It is not something the average male could *possibly* anticipate when he asks a woman out for the very first time. If he had any inkling, he would never, ever ask. Maybe that's why God made the process of *getting* pregnant so enthralling for men. He decided there simply *must* be something spectacular in it for them to counteract that view.

The doctors finally began the extraction of Baby Flintstone. Fred held my hand and smiled down at me on my stainless steel raft. This wasn't the "natural"

scenario either of us had hoped for, but here we were nonetheless. It was like being strapped to a scary roller coaster and there's nothing left to do but throw up your hands and enjoy the ride. A C-section was not what I hoped for, but I guess us small-hipped gals just have to accept the fact that being petite has its price.

I looked back into Fred's kind face. Even though the surgical mask covered his mouth, his Irish eyes smiled so warmly I could feel it. I couldn't fathom this look of adoration. After all, I'd made a mess of the whole Mother Earth gig. Now I was going to have a scar on my belly the size of the San Andreas fault-line.

I also looked like a complete mess. My make-up was gone, my teeth were scuzzy, and my hair was a sweaty disaster, something I could easily see in the reflection of his saucer-sized glasses. As he often does, Fred placated me by saying, "Your hair looks great. Doesn't that count for something?" I smiled back at him, knowing it was a lie. It was the first smile my heart had been able to summon since the word "failure" had floated through the air.

What was taking so long? That darn caterpillar kept crawling across my upper lip, and I begged the anesthesiologist to scratch my nose since I couldn't do it myself. Feeling tired and impatient, I was tempted to say, "It might be faster if you pull the baby out through my nose. That way I wouldn't have a scar, *and* it would scratch my nose on the way out." I managed to suppress my inner I-really-want-to-say-this-but-I-know-I-shouldn't tendency. Even Smart Alecs know it's *not at all smart* to mouth off to people who are taking care of you, particularly when they have a scalpel in their hand.

A few moments later, I heard what sounded like the bleating of a tiny lamb. "It's a boy!" Fred echoed loudly, repeating the doctor's proclamation. I wasn't surprised at all.

After cutting the cord, Fred proudly held up our slimy new son for me to see. "Wow, he's really purple," was my deadpan reply, not expecting such a deep shade of violet. I knew babies came out that color, but it's a little disturbing when it's your own flesh and blood. Within a few seconds the eggplant hue transformed into a nice mottled pink, a much more palatable color on a newborn.

I counted ceiling tiles while the surgical team closed up Uterine Shop. As the neonatal team sized our new son up, Fred bellowed baby statistics from five feet away as though I were on the moon. "Eight pounds, six ounces! Twenty-one inches! Ten fingers! Ten toes!" he thundered over to me with all the power of Zeus. I breathed a sigh of relief.

Two of everything that was supposed to come in pairs, and one of everything else, all perfectly formed. Thank you, Jesus. With news like that, Fred's volume didn't bother me at all. It almost sounded like music. Almost.

Fred was giddy with excitement as he wheeled our son to my bedside. He assumed I would be chomping at the bit to hold our little bundle. I staunchly refused. The C-section had left me tired, weak, and shaky. "What if I drop him and start this whole thing off on the wrong foot?" I thought. I already had "failure to progress" on my permanent hospital record. I wasn't about to have "failure to hold" on there as well.

Tell me, what mother has ever dropped her child and went on to receive a string of tear-jerking Hallmark cards with glowing accolades like "*You're the Greatest Mom Ever* " scribbled across them? Those cards were reserved for the *really great* mothers, the kind who played with life-like dolls, and wanted to be mommies from the time they were five.

I could only surmise that Hallmark carried a completely separate line of cards for the rest of us. They were only available "in the back." These were the second-string Mother's Day cards for so-so moms who randomly decided to give motherhood a whirl and let the chips fall where they may. Those cards had slightly less-inspiring sentiments like this:

Roses are red
Violets are blue.
Dropping me on my head
Was a dumb thing to do.

Hapy Muther'z Day
Thanx for nuthin. . .

No way. I wanted the good cards. I'd come too far to blow it now, so I made Fred take the baby to the nursery for the night with the other fresh-squeezed squealers. I told him if he wanted his son to be nursed right away, he was more than welcome to try. But, if he wanted me to do it, he was going to have to wait until I was good and ready.

The next morning I sat up in a chair, frustrated that my belly looked like a giant hot-air balloon with only *half* the air squished out of it. I beg-your-post-partum, but I thought the baby was out. Wasn't my stomach supposed to be *entirely* deflated by now? Why was I still so fat?

Maybe there had been a mishap. I'll bet a nurse shoved a small pillow in there to stop the bleeding and accidentally forgot to take it out. Or perhaps a really short intern wandered in to check for stray sponges, and the doctor sewed me shut before he could escape. Either way, this was not the back-in-my-blue-jeans look I expected a whole twelve hours after delivery. Wilma Flintstone never looked like this.*

---

* *All television does is set women up for disappointment. I decided to throw my tube out the window the minute I got home.*

As I sat contemplating my navel (literally), a nurse walked in holding a tiny bundle. She tentatively asked me if I was ready to hold my son. I'm sure she had heard by now (via the hospital rumor mill) that one of her own, a supposed "people person," didn't even want to hold her son after she "failed" to give birth the "natural" way. In my mind, I couldn't fail any more than I already had. So without hesitation, I spoke four simple words in the general direction of the doorway.

"Hi Spencer, it's Mommy."

The moment I said it, that tiny pink head, which was barely sticking out from the blanket, began to move. With steady determination, that tiny little head was craning toward me, twisting around slowly until it could twist no more. By the time he was done, my son had turned his perfect little head 180 degrees, so that his dark blue eyes could rest squarely on my face.

At first I thought to myself, "Geez lady, you could have at least turned around to make it easier for him." (And I thought *I* was heartless.) On second thought, I was glad the nurse didn't move a muscle. This way, there was no mistaking his intention.

What I had just witnessed was my son turning his tiny little head in my direction for one simple reason. He recognized my voice, and he was *looking for me.*

My breath stopped. In that one singular moment, it hit me; this little person and I were not strangers meeting for the very first time. In fact, the two of us had been inseparable for the better part of a year. Our hearts had been beating in perfect sync, and his budding little ears had been privy to every word every laugh, and yes, even every prayer murmured in private.

When his gaze finally met mine, the message was clear:

I know you.

I need you.

I love you.

It was a look of pure adoration and simple trust. There was no expectation, no judgment, and not a trace of disappointment anywhere.

He wasn't looking for perfection or self-sufficiency. He had no idea which way was north, and could have cared less that I didn't either. (He would care *later* when I couldn't get him to the right ball field on time, but that's another story for another day.)

His eyes told me that he had no concept of how much I weighed, how long my legs were, or that I was disappointed in both. He had no qualms about his less-than-"natural" arrival, and would never classify his birth as a "failure" in any way.

Suddenly, checking all those boxes didn't seem so important. I wasn't worried that my house was a mess any more, or that I didn't like to clean. It was no longer such a big deal that our yard wasn't immaculate, or that our garage floor was slippery and still smelled strongly of oil.

It wasn't even important that my hair was a mess, which was a good thing. I'll be honest, my hair really only looks good five or six days a year, when it has been cut and styled by a professional. The rest of the time, I don't even do the back because if I can't see it to enjoy it, I might as well not bother. All that didn't matter to this little guy. In his misty blue eyes I saw a completely new reflection of myself, and it had absolutely nothing to do with outward beauty.

For the first time, I realized that it did not matter if I was Greek or Japanese, curly-headed or bald. The only thing that mattered to him was that I was there. And I was.

He didn't need to see my report card, my pay stub, or my family tree. He didn't care what kind of grades I got, how much money I had, or that I had no royal lineage to speak of. All he wanted to see was the face behind that voice, and to know that she was near. And I was.

He didn't even seem to know that I was scared to death about becoming a mother. All he needed me to be was *his* mother, and to love him. And I did.

♥

It was a special kind of love at first sight; a love between two needy human beings who needed each other more than they knew.

♥

I closed my eyes, and laughed.

Afterword

It's a Never Ending
~~Laugh Till You Leak~~
Story

You've gotten this far, so I guess I can safely assume you haven't slipped into a coma while reading. Either that, or you flipped to the back of the book to see if there was an apology somewhere. I hope not. Either way, I want to thank you for taking the time to read my story. It is an honor that you would do so, and I truly mean that.

I learned so much about myself through writing this manuscript. I laughed at myself a lot too, a healthy and humbling exercise. I highly recommend it. Mostly, I came away thankful that being clueless is not illegal, or I would have spent my entire childhood in juvenile detention.

I have come to love the process of writing. Once I got going, it was hard to know where to end the story, because real life is a living, breathing manuscript. It is never truly "finished."* The same is true with parenthood.

Ironically, there are *many* similarities between being a first-time writer, and a first-time parent. How is that, you ask? (I knew you would be dying to know.)

- *You have no idea what you're doing.*

- *You wonder if you're up to the task.*

- *Part way through, you realize you should have wondered harder.*

- *You ignore a lot of great advice you wish you hadn't.*

- *You realize you greatly underestimated the amount of time and energy it would take to see it through.*

- *You have no guarantee of success, even with all that time and energy put into it.*

- *You'll always find something you could have done better.*

- *Other people will also find something you could have done better.*

- *People get tired of hearing you talk about it.*

- *You gain a huge appreciation for everyone who's done it before, and lived to tell about it.*

---

* *Fair warning; do not attempt to write a book unless your family loves frozen pizza. Lots of it.*

Oh, and one other thing…

> *- You hope that if your life story is ever made into a movie,*
> *you are played by a stunning actress who makes you look*
> *way better onscreen than you do in real life.*

Everyone has a story. Mine is no more special than anyone else's. I simply wanted to say this:

If you have ever questioned what it means to be valuable, worthy, beautiful or cherished, you are not the only one who has struggled with that.

If you have ever felt alone, as though every-one around you knows what's going on and you don't, I understand. It's not just you. We've all been there at one point or another.

If you have ever been disappointed in your relationships, your work, your hair, or your station in life, take heart. You are in good company.

If you have ever wondered why you are not inclined toward parenthood while others are, you are not the only one who has wrestled with that indecision. If you doubt your ability to be a good parent, you are not the first, and you certainly won't be the last. Even if you never questioned your parental competency before delivery, no doubt you've had your share of insecurities after the epidural wore off. We all have; and there is tremendous comfort in knowing that you are not alone.

We all have insecurities. For me, the prospect of motherhood put those insecurities under a great big emotional microscope. Bringing a child into the world is a huge responsibility. If you think about it, parenthood is one of the few things in life that is permanent (well, that and tattoos, but that's a topic for my next book).

You can run away from home, drop out of school, quit your job, sell your possessions, even legally divorce your spouse; but you will never, ever stop being someone's parent once you go down that road. It is forever. That alone should give one pause for thought (or reason to panic).

It is also something we have to be able to laugh together about. I am all for being a responsible parent, but let's face it; we are going to flub up from time to time no matter how hard we try. It's human nature.

Part of becoming a parent entails dragging all the baggage we have from childhood into the delivery room, and inadvertently dumping it on our kid the minute they're born. It is then up to the poor little dear, to sort through it for the rest of their life.

Our grandparents did it to their kids. Our parents did it to us. We will do it to our children, and they will do it to theirs. Some of it they will keep. Some of it they will throw away. Some of it they will marry.

That, my dear friends, is the *real* circle of life.

On a personal note (ok, so this whole book has been one big personal note, but this part is *really* personal), I would like to share something from my heart.

Writing this memoir was a unique form of time travel. It gave me the unexpected ability to watch my younger self slowly develop on paper, like a photograph develops in a darkroom. (For all you digital youngsters, ask a docent at the Smithsonian what a darkroom is.)

It was a bit like being a mother watching her child grow up. Sometimes I giggled at the antics of the little girl in the story, wondering what in the world she was thinking. Yet, at other times, I wanted to scoop her up and love on her, with words of comfort, encouragement, and compassion.

As I watched the girl grow into a teenager and then a young woman, it hurt to see her churn with so much insecurity and self-doubt. I found myself wishing I could go back in time and offer a few life-changing messages that could have spared my earlier self so much grief and uncertainty.

First of all, I would tell her that perfection was overrated. Reaching for it would only lead to disappointment and heartache.

Next, I would hug her and tell her she was beautiful. She never grasped that. I would warn her that the never-ending quest for physical beauty can rob a person's soul like nothing else. (I would also encourage her to enjoy the weight she was at the time, because one day she would look back and give her right arm to be that weight again.)

That impressionable young lady understood that words from those we love carry a lot of weight. What she didn't recognize, was that people, especially parents, are just fallible human beings doing the best they know how. She would hope her own children would understand that someday.

I would also go back in time and tell that scared young wife not to be afraid of becoming a mom. I wanted to inform her that there are no perfect children and no perfect parents, only a perfect God with a perfect plan. She desperately needed to be reminded that she could rest in Him, the only One who is fully capable of handling all our shortcomings, our insecurities, and ultimately, our disappointments.

Finally, I would go back in time to reassure that precious girl that she never was, and never would be, alone. I would tell her to pray more and worry less. She was going to be okay, and so were her children. ♥

Made in the USA
Columbia, SC
09 February 2021